Passport's Illustrated Travel Guide to

SAN FRANCISCO

FROM
**THOMAS
COOK**
AA

PASSPORT BOOKS
a division of *NTC Publishing Group*
Lincolnwood, Illinois USA

CLOS PEGASE

Published by Passport Books,
a division of NTC Publishing Group,
4255 W. Touhy Avenue,
Lincolnwood (Chicago), Illinois
60646-1975 U.S.A.

Written by Nigel Tisdall

Original photography by Ken Paterson

Edited, designed and produced by AA Publishing.
© The Automobile Association 1997.
Maps © The Automobile Association 1997.

Library of Congress Catalog Card Number: 95-73294

ISBN 0-8442-4827-4

The contents of this publication are believed correct at the time of
printing. Nevertheless, the publishers cannot accept responsibility for
any errors or omissions, or for changes in the details given in this guide
or for the consequences of any reliance on the information provided by
the same. Assessments of attractions, hotels, restaurants, and so forth are
based upon the author's own experience and therefore descriptions given
in this guide necessarily contain an element of subjective opinion which
may not reflect the publisher's opinion or dictate a reader's own
experiences on another occasion.
**We have tried to ensure accuracy in this guide, but things do
change and we would be grateful if readers would advise us of any
inaccuracies they may encounter.**

Published by Passport Books in conjunction with AA Publishing and the
Thomas Cook Group Ltd.

Color separation: BTB Colour Reproduction, Whitchurch, Hampshire,
England.

Printed by: Edicoes ASA, Oporto, Portugal.

Contents

About this Book

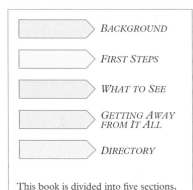

BACKGROUND

FIRST STEPS

WHAT TO SEE

GETTING AWAY
FROM IT ALL

DIRECTORY

This book is divided into five sections,
identified by the above color coding

Savoring the view from Twin Peaks (below);
Golden Gate Promenade by Fort Point (right)

The **Background** gives an introduction
to the city – its history, geography,
politics, culture.
First Steps offers practical advice on
arriving and getting around.
What to See is an alphabetical listing of
places to visit, divided into two regions
and interspersed with walks and tours.
Getting Away from It All highlights
places off the beaten track where it's
possible to relax and enjoy peace and
quiet.
Finally the **Directory** provides practical
information – from shopping and
entertainment to children and sports,
including a section on business matters.
Special highly illustrated features on
specific aspects of the city appear
throughout the book.

BACKGROUND

"If you can't find what you're
looking for in San Francisco,
you just ain't looking."
TREVOR HAILEY,
1993

Introduction

You hear such good things about San Francisco; it's bound to make a first-time visitor sceptical. Mention its name and invariably up pops a stock image of cable cars cruising a switchback of hills. In the background the fog is swirling around Golden Gate Bridge, ferries are zipping across the Bay to Alcatraz, popcorn-munching children are laughing at the clowns on Fisherman's Wharf ...

Those shots in the tourist brochures don't lie, but neither do they give the whole picture. San Francisco is indeed a city heaven-made for a vacation – congenial, compact, walkable, with rewarding historical and cultural sights, a knock-out restaurant scene, elegant hotels, and enough theater, nightlife and sports to please the most cosmopolitan traveler.

The views of San Francisco Bay from its panoramic hills are terrific, the weather is dramatic, there are vast, mature parks and long, romantic sands. Drive north across the soul-enhancing Golden Gate Bridge, head south down Highway 1, and you're immediately into scenic California, lost for choice between

Stalls selling locally caught Dungeness crabs are a good reason to visit Fisherman's Wharf

serene redwood forests, lonely shorelines and bucolic wine valleys. Everything, in short, is here to guarantee San Francisco's position as one of the world's favorite vacation destinations.

> "You wouldn't think that such a place as San Francisco could exist. The wonderful sunlight there, the hills, the great bridges, the Pacific at your shoes. Beautiful Chinatown. Every race in the world."
> Dylan Thomas

But that's not what makes it so astonishingly popular, the sort of place where Tony Bennett could leave his heart and which sees new settlers arriving daily by plane, train and Greyhound, looking for peace and the chance to kick a few dreams into place. For San Francisco is not so much a city as a phenomenon, a collective wish born in a gold rush, built on a fault line, framed by the bright blue Bay only discovered in 1769.

Optimists have been heading here for a century and a half now, rolling in like the Pacific fog that dances so famously through its skyscrapers. From the air the city looks as neat as the inside of a transistor radio: pockets of ornate Victorian housing, strips of seaside

Beautiful city: the view from Buena Vista Park to Golden Gate Bridge and the Marin Headlands

suburbia, boxed-up parks and question mark freeways sweep up to a reach-for-the-sky Financial District bejeweled with art deco skyscrapers and mirror-glassed extravagance.

Down on the streets the big sound is immigrant energy – an intoxicating cultural mixture with distinct Italian, Chinese, Hispanic, Japanese and southeast Asian neighborhoods set in a spicy soup of diverse Californian lifestyles.

This is the city that gave us the Beats, hippy revolution, gay militancy and yuppies (a term first coined in the Bay area). It doesn't mind where you sit on the gender rainbow, whether you like rock or Frank Sinatra, ballet or roller-blading, if you're here to lunch naked on the beach or take the kids to Alcatraz. Welcome to America's most tolerant city – it's one of the greatest in the world.

The city's beginnings

To protect themselves from the encroaching British and Russians, a Spanish army expedition set out in 1769 on what would result in a string of missions being established by the Franciscan order. It could be said, therefore, than San Francisco's history only started with the founding of the Mission of San Francisco de Asis (better known as Mission Dolores) in 1776 at the cove then known as Yerba Buena (literally "good grass"). It was not the only mission to be set up around the bay. To protect their interests, the Spanish instigated the missions of San Jose, Santa Clara, San Rafael, and San Francisco de Solano at Sonoma.

The settlement remained little more than a village until the discovery of gold at Sutter's sawmill in the Sierra's.

Geography

*B*ounded by the Pacific Ocean and the Bay, San Francisco stands at the northern tip of a peninsula formed by the Santa Cruz mountains. The city covers 47 square miles and has approximately 724,000 citizens, making it one of the most densely populated cities in the United States.

CALIFORNIA

American Plate travels westward. The earthquake that devastated the city in 1906 was caused when subterranean pressures forced the Pacific Plate to suddenly leap forward 20 feet.

Landscape

San Francisco is draped across 43 hills, three of which – Twin Peaks, Mount Davidson and Mount Sutro – rise above 900 feet. Much land has been reclaimed from the Bayside shoreline, a process that began in 1849 when hundreds of ships were abandoned in the harbor by eager gold prospectors.

The beauty of the city owes much to its parks, in particular the 1,017-acre Golden Gate Park which slices through the west of the city. Many other beaches, headlands and islands come under the jurisdiction of the Golden Gate National Recreation Area (GGNRA). Its soothing empire recently benefited from the addition of the 1,480-acre Presidio, one of the oldest military outposts in the US.

The Bay

San Francisco Bay is one of the best natural ports in America. Fed by 16 rivers, it covers 400 square miles and joins with the sea at the three-mile-long strait of the Golden Gate. The Bay is actually a drowned river valley – its waters are 318 feet deep beneath the Golden Gate Bridge but only 100 feet under the eastern section of the Bay Bridge. Seventy per cent of it is less than 12 feet deep.

Geology

San Francisco lies close to the San Andreas Fault zone that runs the length of California and marks the division between the Pacific and North American tectonic plates. The Pacific Plate moves northwestward about two inches every year, while the slower moving North

Economy

Ever since the Gold Rush, San Francisco has been a city of service industries. From supplying prospectors with tools and then banking their gold, it has developed into a thriving commercial and financial center that is now home to the Pacific Stock Exchange and the headquarters of many of America's leading banks and insurance companies.

In the past the port of San Francisco

A road winds up to the panoramic summit of Twin Peaks, one of the highest of San Francisco's hills

was kept busy with traditional sea-based industries such as whaling, fishing and shipbuilding, and its fortunes were boosted by the opening of the Panama Canal in 1914 and naval activity during World War II. Now it is in decline, and its piers increasingly given over to tourism and leisure. Visitors coming to the city on vacation or business have become a crucial component of San Francisco's economy, generating an annual turnover of over $4 billion.

Bay Area

Six million people live in the San Francisco metropolitan region, the fifth largest in the country. The area covers nine counties and extends north to the wine country of Napa and Sonoma, south to San Jose and Silicon Valley, and east to Alameda and Contra Costa Counties.

People

San Francisco and the Bay Area boasts one of the most ethnically diverse communities in the United States. Around 50 percent of the region's residents are non-white, while over a quarter of San Franciscans are of Asian or Pacific background – a classic example of "melting pot" America.

History

18,000BC–AD1500

Migrants from Asia cross the Bering Strait and populate the Americas. By the 16th century around 1½ million native Indians are spread across the United States, including 13,000 Miwoks and Ohlones in the Bay Area.

1579

Sailing up the Californian coast in the *Golden Hind*, Sir Francis Drake misses the entrance to San Francisco Bay. Landing at Drake's Bay in Marin County, he claims the land of Nova Albion for Queen Elizabeth I of England.

1769

Traveling overland, a Spanish expedition led by Gaspar de Portolá discovers the Bay of San Francisco. Over the next 54 years a string of 21 colonial missions are established between San Diego and Sonoma.

1775

The first ship sails into San Francisco Bay. Within a year the Spanish have founded the Presidio (fort) and a Mission named in honour of St Francis of Assisi.

1821

Mexico declares its independence from Spain and encourages its citizens to settle in northern California.

1835

An English sea captain, William Richardson, founds the small town of Yerba Buena (Good Herb), which attracts an influx of American settlers.

1846

The United States declares war on Mexico. In Sonoma, the Bear Flag Revolt proclaims the short-lived (but long-remembered) independent republic of California. The USS *Portsmouth* sails into Yerba Buena, seizing the town for the Union and renaming it San Francisco.

1848

Gold is discovered in the Sacramento Valley. Thousands of prospectors rush to California, most through the port of San Francisco.

1850

California becomes the 31st State of the Union with its capital in San Jose (later moved to Sacramento). Within two years the population of San Francisco has grown to 25,000.

1869

The Central Pacific Railroad links San Francisco with the East Coast. Seven years later the Southern Pacific Railroad connects it with Los Angeles.

Murals from the 1915 Panama-Pacific Exposition

Damage from the violent earthquake of 1906

Construction is mostly carried out by immigrant Chinese labor.

1870
Founding of Golden Gate Park.

1873
The world's first cable car trundles down Clay Street.

1906
An earthquake and ensuing fires devastate the city.

1915
The Panama-Pacific International Exposition celebrates the opening of the Panama Canal.

1933
Alcatraz Island becomes a Federal Penitentiary. Public works projects such as the Coit Tower provide employment during the Great Depression.

1936–7
Opening of the Bay Bridge and the Golden Gate Bridge.

1939
Golden Gate International Exposition on Treasure Island attracts 17 million visitors.

1941–51
The US enters World War II in 1941 after the Japanese attack on Pearl Harbor. San Francisco becomes the hub of military operations in the Pacific. In 1945 the original United Nations Charter is signed in the War Memorial Opera House, and in 1951 the Treaty marking the end of hostilities with Japan.

1950s
During the Cold War, San Francisco emerges as a haven for the Beat Generation, an artistic reaction to the conformity of post-war America.

1960s
In 1963 the prison on Alcatraz closes, and in 1967 hippies fill the streets of Haight-Ashbury for the "Summer of Love." Protests against the US entry into the Vietnam War (1954–75) and campaigns for gay rights bring the Bay Area a reputation as a centre of liberal and counter-cultural activity.

1970s
In 1972 the Golden Gate National Recreation Area is created, and two years later the BART (Bay Area Rapid Transit) links San Francisco and Oakland. The Castro emerges as the centre of the city's growing gay community.

1980s
AIDS surfaces. In 1989 the worst earthquake since 1906 strikes, killing more than 60 people in the Bay Area.

1994
The Presidio is incorporated into the Golden Gate National Recreation Area.

1995
The 49ers football team win the Superbowl. San Francisco welcomes 13 million visitors a year.

THE GOLD RUSH

On 24 January 1848 James Marshall, a carpenter constructing a sawmill at Coloma, on the western slopes of the Sierra Nevada mountains, discovered nuggets of gold in the American River. His find triggered one of the most dramatic human migrations in history, and put San Francisco firmly on the world map.

Within a few months amateur prospectors were rushing to California in their thousands. Some travelled

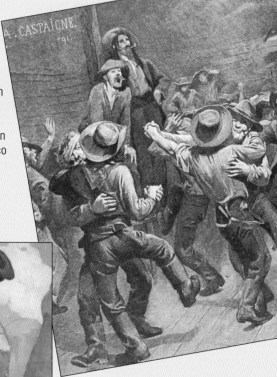

Lucky prospectors (left) celebrated in the city's saloons (above)

overland in wagon trains from the East Coast, but the majority arrived by sea via Panama or the Cape Horn. In 1849, the year when the miners were christened "Forty-niners," 40,000 optimists sailed into San Francisco Bay. Even the ships' crews rushed off to the gold fields, leaving the harbor at Yerba Buena clogged with abandoned vessels

arrived in 1853 and started kitting miners out with durable blue canvas trousers.

In 1859 silver was discovered in western Nevada, reviving San Francisco's role as a gateway to riches. By then mining had become commercialized, creating a tycoon class that helped rebuild the city in grand style. Their ostentatious mansions crowned Nob Hill, which remains the most desirable address in the city. Evocative mementoes of those pioneer times can be seen in the Wells Fargo History Museum (see page 90–1).

The legacy of the Gold Rush has been far-reaching – from the gay community's supposed roots in the almost exclusively male

Historic gold in the Wells Fargo Museum

that were incorporated into the rapidly growing town.

While a few struck gold, many fortune hunters fell victim to swindlers and profiteers. By the end of the 1850s San Francisco had become a lawless boom town that fulfilled every Wild West cliché, an unromantic tale of saloons and whorehouses, gambling dens and vigilante gangs. According to *The Sacramento Union* newspaper, there were 1,400 murders in six years. The smart money, as ever, was in supply. Real and lasting fortunes were made by people like Levi Strauss, a hard-working German immigrant who

population of the city 150 years ago, to executives who only half-joke that Wild West values persist in the Financial District. San Francisco is and always will be a city of fortune-seekers.

Culture

San Franciscans

Your chances of meeting someone who can genuinely claim to be born, bred and still living in the midst of San Francisco are not good. This is "a destination," where everyone comes from somewhere else and most genuine locals are either concentrated in ethnic neighborhoods, or have defected to the suburbs and other Bay Area towns.

As the North Beach poet Lawrence Ferlinghetti put it, San Francisco is where "the frontier first got tamed." The city is demographically unusual because the Gold Rush attracted two types of immigrants simultaneously – Americans racing overland from the East and ship-borne Europeans who had no experience of the Yankee way of doing things.

Unlike the pioneer farmers and ranchers that traditionally settled the West, they came from all classes and backgrounds.

The result is a city of undying immigrant ambition, where brave new hopes are grafted on to cherished memories of the old country. San Franciscans are justly proud of their multicultural diversity and tolerance of other people's lifestyles, and exude a spirit of getting along that other cities probably only enjoy in times of war. And, perhaps because the Big 'Quake could happen at any moment, they never forget that life is about having a good time.

Murals in the Mission: street paintings are a commentary on life in San Francisco

Art

The opening of the San Francisco Museum of Modern Art in 1995 confirmed the city's credentials as the art capital of the West. Its cultural

Culture for all: world class ballet (above) and the music of the streets

pedigree stretches back to 1871 and the founding of the San Francisco Art Institute, now located in Chestnut Street, which has played an influential role in the development of art in the Bay Area. Many of the city's commercial galleries can be found close to the Financial District in Sutter, Post and Grant Streets.

Music and dance

San Francisco's first opera house opened in 1851, and the present War Memorial Opera House in Civic Center was the first municipally owned venue in America. Both the San Francisco Opera and the San Francisco Symphony Orchestra have a good reputation, while the San Francisco Ballet is the oldest professional company in the United States. There is also a vigorous interest in modern and ethnic dance.

The city will always be known for its Sixties sounds that became a backing track for the hippy revolution. Legendary performers like Janis Joplin, Jefferson Airplane and The Grateful Dead played Golden Gate Park and the still functioning Fillmore Auditorium, while the naming of the Bill Graham Civic

Auditorium in the Civic Center pays tribute to the promoter who virtually invented the modern rock concert. San Franciscans also have a penchant for enjoying big feelings in small clubs – jazz and blues both flourished in North Beach venues and now inspire respected annual festivals, while SoMa (the area south of Market Street) is renowned for its hip dance clubs.

Education

The intellectual life of the Bay Area has always been dominated by the world class universities at Stanford and Berkeley. Their academic achievements, sporting rivalry and shared history of student activism have tended to obscure San Francisco's own educational institutions. The oldest of these is the University of San Francisco, located near the northeast corner of Golden Gate Park. Founded in 1855 and still run by Jesuits, the twin towers of its St Ignatius Church are a familar landmark in the west of the city. Further south near Mount Sutro, the University of California San Francisco dates from 1899 and is known in particular for its medical research.

WRITERS AND POETS

"I do not know," Anthony Trollope declared in 1875, "that in all my travels I visited a city less interesting." Whatever writers have to say about San Francisco, it is rarely bland. The city has inspired a feast of novels, poetry and high-octane journalism that provides an engrossing chronicle of its moods and moments.

Like the early San Franciscans, many authors were roving fortune hunters themselves. Mark Twain (1835–1910) moved to the city in 1864 after a fruitless stab at gold prospecting (recalled in *Roughing It*), while the love of a married woman brought an impecunious Robert Louis Stevenson (1850–94) to a garret in Bush Street in 1879. Jack London (1876–1916), born in Oakland, dropped out of Berkeley to join the Klondike Gold Rush, and concluded a life of volatile wandering by building a home in Glen Ellen, Sonoma. Amongst his frenetic output is a gripping eye-witness account of the 1906 earthquake.

San Francisco life is also recorded in depth in works by Frank Norris

(1870–1902) and Ambrose Bierce (1842–1914), who both worked for local newspapers, while Dashiell Hammett (1894–1961), the guru of hard-boiled detective fiction, lived in the city center for most of the 1920s.

He can be held responsible for the city's image as a badly lit playground for back-alley sleuths – the first Sam Spade novel, *The Maltese Falcon*, was completed in 1929.

In the 1950s, as writers like Jack Kerouac and Allen Ginsberg challenged literary and social orthodoxies, San Francisco developed a reputation as America's Poetry Corner. Lawrence Ferlinghetti opened the City Lights Bookstore on North Beach, Ginsberg read *Howl* and the Beat Generation was born. The following decade saw San

Francisco become the center of the hippy world, and its drug-fuelled highs and lows were vividly chronicled by writers like Tom Wolfe and Hunter S Thompson.

More recently, Armistead Maupin's *Tales from the City*, Vikram Seth's epic narrative poem *The Golden Gate*, and the novels of American-Chinese authors Amy Tan and Maxine Hong Kingston, have continued the story of San Francisco.

Jack London's cabin in Oakland (left); Jack Kerouac Street (right) and the adjacent City Lights bookstore (below)

JACK KEROUAC STREET

On January 25, 1988 The City of San Francisco approved a proposal by CITY LIGHTS BOOKS to rename 12 streets for S.F. writers and artists including this alley.

CITY LIGHTS Booksellers & Publishers

CITY LIGHTS BOOKS

Politics

*P*olitics in San Francisco is never dull, and few visitors pass through the city without being at least warmed by the burning issues of the day.

To an outsider, San Francisco appears a deeply politicized city, a bastion of liberalism in a state where right wing policies rule. Officially the city's political dramas are played out in the Civic Center, where the chief characters are the Mayor, the 11-strong Board of Supervisors, and the various constituencies they must answer to come reelection time.

Politics in San Francisco means much more than voting for flag-waving parties though. Issues of gender, race and the environment steal the front pages as often as crime and the economy do in other cities. This is the town that gave us hippy freedoms and gay rights, where the cogs of the democratic process are openly displayed and Utopia is being constructed by the Golden Gate. It's looking good so far, but visitors should know that it just isn't safe to walk the streets without carrying opinions – so get some quick, on vagrancy tickets for the homeless, Draconian anti-smoking laws and "three strikes and out" sentences for repeated offenders.

San Francisco recently elected its first African-American mayor Willie Brown, a Democrat, who replaced the controversial Frank Jordan.

City Hall is San Francisco's political stage (left); mural in North Beach (right)

EMPEROR NORTON I
The true story of Joshua A Norton typifies the buccaneering people politics of San Francisco. One day in 1854, after falling into sudden bankruptcy, this proud English merchant appeared in Montgomery Street wearing imperial military uniform. He informed the *San Francisco Bulletin* that he was the Emperor of the United States and Protector of Mexico. The city conspired to believe him for the next 25 years – minting a special Norton currency, printing his proclamations, and inviting the Emperor to top restaurants and theatrical first nights. When he died in 1880 thousands of loyal subjects attended his funeral.

FIRST STEPS

"It's an odd thing, but anyone
who disappears is said to have
been seen in San Francisco.
It must be a delightful city and
possess all the attractions of
the next world."

OSCAR WILDE,
1882

First Steps

ORIENTATION

San Francisco is built on a grid pattern
of streets that takes little notice of the
major hills underneath. Two of the
widest sit on the map like a pair of
dividers and will soon become familiar –
the diagonal Market Street and the
north–south Van Ness Avenue. Most
hotels, and popular areas such as the
Financial District, North Beach and
Fisherman's Wharf, lie within the
northeast quadrant of the city enclosed
by these streets. The surrounding
neighborhoods and parks have much to
offer too – for a perfect introduction to
the complete city follow the 49-Mile
Scenic Drive (see pages 106–7).

Road signs help visitors find their way around
San Francisco's diverse neighborhoods

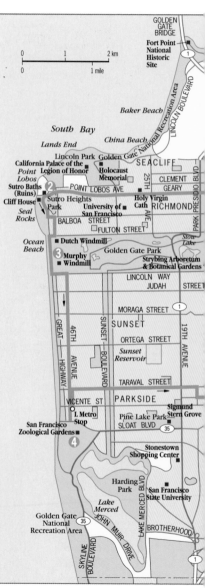

SAN FRANCISCO

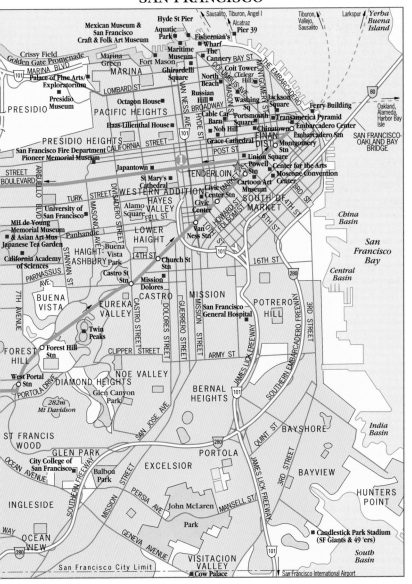

Cable cars are not only a tourist attraction but a fun way to travel round the city

ARRIVING

Most visitors arrive by air at San Francisco International Airport, 14 miles south of the city center. A shuttle bus is the quickest way to get to your accommodations – the journey takes about 30 minutes, sometimes longer in rush hour. See pages 178–9.

GETTING AROUND
Cable cars

San Francisco's three cable car routes are a city trademark (see pages 26–7). The two most popular lines, Powell/Hyde and Powell/Mason, start from a turntable by Hallidie Plaza, at the junction of Powell and Market Streets. At peak times long lines can form here and at other termini. Your chances won't improve by walking up to the next stop, so tough it out as best you can or try to adopt an alternative strategy – such as riding the cars early in the morning, in the evening, or taking the less-crowded California Street line. See pages 100–1.

Driving

You don't need a car to see the city's main sights – buses, cable cars and taxis can get you anywhere. However, the use of a vehicle for a few days will allow you to follow the 49-Mile Drive and take day trips to Muir Woods, the Napa and Sonoma wine valleys or tour the Bay. When planning journeys try to avoid the weekday rush hours, which generally peak between 7am and 9am, and 5pm and 6pm.

Public transport

MUNI (San Francisco Municipal Railway) operate a complex but comprehensive public transport network reaching all corners of the city. It is worth befriending the bus system as this is a cheap and reliable way to enjoy San Francisco – see page 102 for a suggested ride. In addition there are five MUNI metro lines with streetcars that run underground in the city center and on the surface in outlying parts.

Travel on MUNI is efficient but impersonal – a bus ride is $1 (children 35¢) and drivers don't give change. It will probably be economical to buy a MUNI Passport, valid for 1, 3 or 7 days, which allows unlimited travel on buses, metro lines and cable cars, as well as offering discounted admission to some museums and sights. These can be bought from the Visitor Center in Hallidie Plaza and other outlets, along with the useful MUNI *Street and Transit Map*.
MUNI Information, tel: 415/673–6864.

BART (Bay Area Rapid Transit) provides speedy access by rail to the Bay Area and has shared stops with the MUNI metro stations in Market Street. You'll need a handful of coins and some patience for the ticket machines.
BART Information, tel: 417/788–2278.

Ferry services are geared to the needs of commuters as well as tourists, and are an exhilarating way to enjoy San Francisco Bay. See page 132 for details.

As is often true elsewhere taxis are reasonably priced and ubiquitous except

Buses are a cheap and easy way to get around

when it's raining, cold or you need one in a hurry. Hotels are the best place to start looking – at night book one by phone rather than hang around in the street looking hopeful.
Veteran's Taxicab Company, tel: 415/552–1300.

For public transport maps and further information see pages 186–7.

Combined MUNI and BART stops

HOW TO BE A LOCAL

* Learn how to drive during rush hour
* Don't visit the city parks at night
* Remember that only gauche out-of-towners call it "Frisco"
* Say "The Mark" not "The Hopkins"
* Don't try swimming in San Francisco Bay
* View wine drinking as a serious business
* Never call the cable car a trolley
* Know the difference between an espresso and a latte
* Be laid back, but stylishly
* Don't admit that you might go sightseeing in Oakland.
* Be prepared for frequent change of weather in the same afternoon.

FOG

The city's souvenir shops make a nice few bucks selling "I Love San Francisco" sweatshirts to visitors unprepared for the chill mornings of "Fog City." The rest of California might well be full of sun-drenched beaches and fire hazard warnings, but San Francisco has its own exhibitionist micro-climate in summer that brings fog racing through the Golden Gate Bridge like dry ice. Don't be put off: the fog is great fun, a mystical, comforting character that rolls in for a morning chat but has often vanished by mid-afternoon.

Golden Gate Bridge is often veiled by fog

SAFETY

Major earthquakes in 1906 and 1989 (see pages 54–5) are a reminder that San Francisco is built on a fault line. Many new buildings have been constructed to withstand tremors, while older ones carry solemn warnings implying that you are about to shop in a rickety pack of cards, so don't even *think* about post-earthquake litigation. If the earth moves, the official advice is to seek cover, move away from windows, don't use elevators, and don't run outside.

Like all large cities, San Francisco has its share of violent crime. Just be sure to avoid all parks and deserted or poorly lit streets at night, carry no ostentatious valuables and leave nothing you care about in a car. Tourists should avoid straying into the Tenderloin, a rough and depressed area west of Union Square and north of the Civic Center, bounded loosely by O'Farrell, Polk, Mason and Market streets.

SMOKING

As the result of escalating prohibitionary legislation, smokers are made to feel as welcome in San Francisco as lepers at a medieval fair. One of the bizarre sights of the Financial District is the designer-dressed, chain-puffing executives who gather outside the entrances to their smoking-free palaces like naughty schoolkids – a delinquent assembly that has now prompted hectoring signs declaring "No Smoking within 15 feet of this Building."

The message for visitors is plain – if you are a smoker, look before you light up. In most restaurants it is still permissible to smoke at the bar, but in all shops, offices, modes of transport and public areas – including Candlestick Park (recently renamed 3Com Park) – it is

MONEYSAVING TIPS

- buy a MUNI Passport for travel (see page 22)
- if you plan to visit several sights in Golden Gate Park, get a Golden Gate Park Cultural Pass (see page 61)
- buy half-price theater tickets from the TIX Bay Area kiosk in Union Square (see page 144)
- portions in restaurants are often large, so don't order more than you need. You can take what's left away in a "doggy bag"
- free-of-charge San Francisco sights include the Cable Car Barn, Fort Point, Golden Gate Bridge, the Maritime Museum, the Presidio Army Museum, plus vibrant neighborhoods like Chinatown, North Beach and the Mission
- join a free, volunteer-led walk organized by The Friends of San Francisco Library, which covers many historical and cultural aspects of the city. Donations accepted. (See page 30.)
- some museums offer free admission one day in the first week of the month. See individual entries for exact times.

Tuesday – SFMOMA

Wednesday – Asian Art Museum, California Academy of Sciences, California Palace of the Legion of Honor (second week), Exploratorium, Fort Mason Center museums, M H de Young Memorial Museum, San Francisco Zoo

Thursday – Bay Area Discovery Museum, Center for the Arts

Saturday – Asian Art Museum, M H de Young Memorial Museum

forbidden. All hotels now have non-smoking rooms and floors, so make your needs known when you make a reservation.

Any questions? The Visitor Information Center in Market Square can always help

TOURIST INFORMATION

The helpful San Francisco Visitor Information Center is on the lower level of Hallidie Plaza, by the junction of Powell and Market streets and the Powell Street Metro/BART station. *Tel: 415/391–2000. Events Information, tel: 415/391–2001. Open: Monday to Friday 9am–5:30pm, Saturday 9am–3pm, Sunday 10am–2pm.*

CABLE CARS

Devised in 1873 by a Scottish engineer, Andrew Hallidie, San Francisco's world-famous cable car system has survived earthquakes, fires and decades of neglect to become a much-loved tourist attraction that is also a great way to get around.

A wire manufacturer and designer of haulage systems for the gold mines, Hallidie is said to have been spurred to invention after witnessing an accident in which several horses died after their well-laden carriage dragged them back down a steep hill. His first cars, one of which can be seen in the Cable Car Barn and Museum (see page 38), ran along Clay Street. The following year eight more lines were built, and by the end of the decade the network covered 112 miles.

Cable cars operate by gripping on to a continuously moving woven steel cable set in the center of the street, which runs in a loop powered from the Cable Car Barn in Mason Street. A gripman in the center of the car uses a pliers-like lever to control the movement of the car, which runs at an average 9.5mph.

In the early 1980s the entire cable car system was overhauled at a cost of $67 million and only three lines are now operated. The most popular are Powell/Mason and Powell/Hyde, which use one-way cars with a turntable at either end, while the quieter California Street line uses cars with a driver's cab at each end. Each car has a two-person crew who can be as colorful and temperamental as their vehicles.

Though at times San Francisco's cable cars can become overcrowded tourist-traps, they are still used by local commuters, and they provide an irresistible source of inexpensive fairground thrills. Hopping on a vintage wooden car at sunset is like buying a ticket back to city life a century ago.

Who could fail to enjoy that lurching whoosh as you charge down to Fisherman's Wharf with the gripman banging his bell as if the Apocalypse was nigh? Was public transport ever so much fun?

Ancient and modern cars (opposite page); gripman at work (left)

Neighborhoods

San Francisco is a city of diverse neighborhoods, and the opportunity to plunge into many different worlds in the space of a bus ride is a fundamental part of its appeal to both residents and visitors. Neighborhood borders are imprecise, fluctuating with the processes of gentrification and ethnic drift that move through the city, but the following areas all have a tangible identity.

CITY CENTER

The heart of San Francisco is often referred to as simply Downtown, and the majority of the city's shops, offices, theaters and hotels can be found in the grid of streets surrounding Union Square. This is the area where most visitors stay. To its east rise the skyscrapers of the Financial District, and to its west lies the seedy Tenderloin, now home to a growing southeast Asian community. The Beaux-Arts public buildings of the Civic Center fill the corner between Market Street and Van Ness Avenue. The streets to the west of Van Ness Avenue are known as the Western Addition, a mix of historic Victorian housing, severe modern estates and Japantown, the focus of San Francisco's Japanese community.

NORTHEAST

To the north of Downtown lie the busy streets of Chinatown, the traditional home of San Francisco's 85,000 Chinese-American citizens. This is bordered by North Beach, a historic Italian neighborhood with abundant cafés and restaurants. Its main street, Columbus Avenue, is overlooked to the east by Telegraph Hill, capped by the Coit Tower, and to the west by Russian Hill, a smart residential district. Even more exclusive is nearby Nob Hill, its summit crowned with grand hotels and millionaire mansions since the 1880s.

The piers of Fisherman's Wharf surround San Francisco's northeast shore – once devoted to fishing boats and ferries, but now overwhelmed by the tourist trade.

SOUTH OF MARKET STREET

As well as being a main transport artery leading to the Ferry Building, Market Street is a traditional socio-economic dividing line that signals cultural change as rivers do in other major cities. Once an area of light industry and warehousing, SoMa (the area South of Market Street) is becoming gentrified, most noticeably around the arts center of Yerba Buena Gardens and at its east end, where waterfront buildings along the Embarcadero and South Beach have been restored. South of 16th Street, the Mission is the long-standing home of San Francisco's Hispanic population, while the city's gay community is centered on the Castro. Further south lie two predominantly working-class neighborhoods, Potrero Hill and Noe Valley.

WEST

The Marina district, tucked between Fort Mason and the Presidio, is a sports-conscious sidekick of Pacific Heights, San Francisco's premier family neighborhood with good schools, yuppie-packed restaurants and non-stop shopping in Union Street. Richmond, sandwiched between the Presidio and

Boulevard in Sunset: San Francisco is a city of many quaint neighborhoods

Golden Gate Park, is a residential belt of staid, middle-class housing that stretches to Ocean Beach, with Clement Street emerging as a New Chinatown. Its conservative refrains are picked up to the south in Sunset. By contrast Haight-Ashbury, gathered around the Panhandle of Golden Gate Park, has been resolutely alternative since it became a hippy mecca in the Sixties. To its south, the houses hugging the steep slopes of Twin Peaks enjoy the best views of the city.

NEIGHBORHOODS

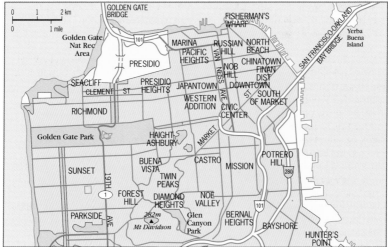

WALKS

Guided walking tours of San Francisco's neighborhoods are highly recommended. Led by locals who know their area inside out, they often include a meal or drink at venues you would never find on your own, and are the best way for a stranger to gain a rapid insight into the city.

AM Walks

Historic early morning walks through Downtown San Francisco with tales of the Barbary Coast and Dashiell Hammett. *Tel: 415/928–5965.*

City Guides

Cultural walks on many themes organized by the Friends of San Francisco Library, including mural tours of the Mission. *Tel: 415/557–4266. Free but donations accepted.*

Cruisin' the Castro

A stroll through San Francisco's gay community. *Tel: 415/550–8110.*

Inside Art Tours

A peek at the Bay Area art world with gallery visits. *Tel: 415/386–1840.*

Rachel's Flower Power Tour

Everything there is to know about Haight-Ashbury past and present. *Tel: 415/221–8442.*

Roger's High Points

Detailed insights into Nob Hill, Chinatown and Golden Gate Bridge. *Tel: 415/742–9611.*

Wok Wiz

Walks around Chinatown with the option of a *dim-sum* lunch. *Tel: 415/355–9657.*

TOURS

Guided tours of the city by small bus or motorized cable car, and Bay Area excursions with a ferry ride or cruise, are offered by many companies who advertise extensively. For scenic flights and boat trips, see pages 130 and 132 respectively.

A Day in Nature

Walks in Muir Woods, Marin and Napa with picnic. Maximum of four. *Tel: 415/673–0548.*

Cable Car Charters

Narrated city tours by motorized cable car. *Tel: 415/922–2425.*

East Bay Tours

Visit Oakland and Berkeley by BART, returning by ferry. *Tel: 510/465–5791.*

Gray Line

Choice of over 20 tours, including city tours, visits to Muir Woods and the Wine Country, Bay cruises. *Tel: 415/558-9400.*

Kent's Convertible Bug Tours

Tour the city or go for a Napa Valley picnic in a classic open-top Volkswagen. Maximum of three. *Tel: 415/561–9155.*

WHAT TO SEE

*"I left my heart in San Francisco.
High on a hill, it calls to me.
To be where little cable cars
climb halfway to the stars."*
TONY BENNETT,
1964

CITY CENTER

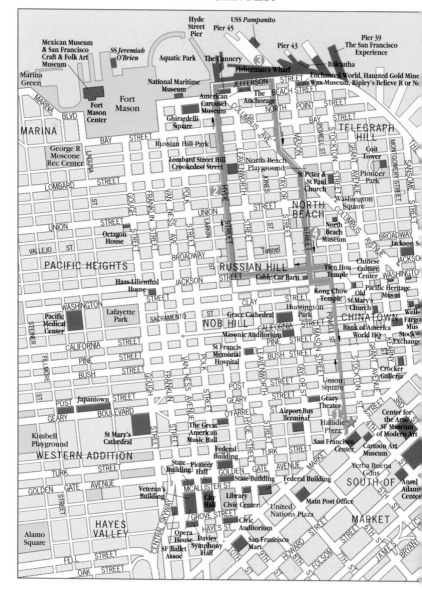

Hyde Street Pier
USS *Pampanito*
Pier 45
Pier 43
Pier 39
The San Francisco Experience
Mexican Museum & San Francisco Craft & Folk Art Museum
SS *Jeremiah O'Brien*
Aquatic Park
The Cannery
Fisherman's Wharf
Balclutha
Marina Green
National Maritime Museum
JEFFERSON STREET
BEACH STREET
Enchanted World, Haunted Gold Mine, Wax Museum, Ripley's Believe It or Not
Fort Mason Center
Fort Mason
American Carousel Museum
The Anchorage
NORTH POINT STREET
BAY STREET
TELEGRAPH HILL
Ghirardelli Square
MARINA
MARINA BLVD
BAY STREET
Russian Hill Park
COLUMBUS AVE
MASON ST
POWELL ST
STOCKTON
GRANT AVENUE
SANSOME STREET
MONTGOMERY
Coit Tower
George R Moscone Rec Center
LAGUNA
Lombard Street Hill Crookedest Street
North Beach Playground
LEAVENWORTH
Pioneer Park
LOMBARD STREET
VAN NESS AVE
POLK STREET
LARKIN
HYDE STREET
JONES
TAYLOR
St Peter & St Paul Church
NORTH BEACH
Washington Square
UNION STREET
UNION STREET
Octagon House
FRANKLIN STREET
GOUGH STREET
North Beach Museum
COLUMBUS AVE
BROADWAY
Jackson St
VALLEJO ST
PACIFIC HEIGHTS
BROADWAY
RUSSIAN HILL
Tunnel
Chinese Culture Center
JACKSON
Haas-Lilienthal House
JACKSON STREET
Cable Car Barn
Tien Hou Temple
Pacific Heritage Mus
WASHINGTON
STEINER
Lafayette Park
SACRAMENTO ST
CLAY STREET
Huntington Park
Grace Cathedral
STREET
Kong Chow Temple
Old St Mary's Church
CHINATOWN
WASHINGTON
Pacific Medical Center
NOB HILL
Masonic Auditorium
CALIFORNIA STREET
POWELL ST
Bank of America World HQ
Wells Fargo Mus
Stock Exchange
CALIFORNIA STREET
FILLMORE
PINE STREET
St Francis Memorial Hospital
VAN NESS
POLK
BUSH STREET
LEAVENWORTH
TAYLOR ST
MASON STREET
STOCKTON ST
GRANT AVENUE
KEARNY
Crocker Galleria
BUSH STREET
POST STREET
Union Square
Japantown
POST STREET
FRANKLIN STREET
GOUGH ST
GEARY STREET
Geary Theater
GEARY BOULEVARD
O'FARRELL ST
Airport Bus Terminal
Hallidie Plaza
3RD STREET
Center for the Arts
SF Museum of Modern Art
Kimbell Playground
St Mary's Cathedral
The Great American Music Hall
HYDE STREET
TURK STREET
San Francisco Center
Cartoon Art Museum
WESTERN ADDITION
Federal Building
State Building
Pioneer Hall
GOLDEN GATE AVENUE
State Building
Federal Building
Yerba Buena Gdns
SOUTH OF
Ansel Adams Center
TURK STREET
Veteran's Building
MCALLISTER ST
Library
Main Post Office
MARKET
GOLDEN GATE AVENUE
City Hall
Civic Center
United Nations Plaza
4TH STREET
5TH STREET
6TH STREET
HAYES VALLEY
GROVE STREET
Civic Auditorium
Alamo Square
Opera House
HAYES ST
Davies Symphony Hall
San Francisco Mart
HOWARD STREET
FOLSOM
JAMES
BRYANT
FELL STREET
SF Ballet Assoc
CENTRAL SKYWAY
7TH STREET
8TH STREET
OAK STREET

Cable Car Line

Sidney Walton Park

Ferry Building

Transamerica Pyramid
Embarcadero Center
Justin Herman Plaza

Golden Gate
Ferry Terminal

us of Money
of the
merican
Vest

Jewish
Museum

Chevron
World
of Oil

Transbay
Terminal
(Greyhound
Bus Depot)

Telephone Pioneer
Communications Mus

Moscone
Convention
Center

China Basin

Southern Pacific Railroad
Terminal

San Francisco

If you only have a short time in San
Francisco, a priority sightseeing list might
include:

- a cable-car ride (see page 100)
- dinner in North Beach (see page 164)
- a boat trip to Alcatraz or Sausalito (see
  page 132)
- a visit to the San Francisco Museum of
  Modern Art (see page 84)
- a walk or cycle ride across the Golden
  Gate Bridge (see pages 58 and 104)
- shopping in Chinatown (see page 46)
- climbing to the top of Coit Tower (see
  page 86)
- taking the kids to the Exploratorium
  (see page 52)
- a visit to the California Academy of
  Sciences and Golden Gate Park (see`
  pages 39 and 60)
- inspecting the historic ships at Hyde
  Street Pier (see page 66)
- driving the 49-Mile Scenic Drive (see
  page 106).

ALCATRAZ

Between 1934 and 1963 the 22-acre rocky island of Alcatraz was home to the most notorious male prison in America, incarcerating legendary criminals such as Al Capone, "Machine Gun" Kelly and Robert Stroud who was canonized by Hollywood as the "Birdman of Alcatraz." Its name comes from the black cormorants (*alcatraces* in Spanish) that sunbathe on its cliffs and rocks – for all its grim history, the island has also served as a wildlife sanctuary attracting brown pelicans, night herons, western gulls and many other birds.

Alcatraz was first fortified in 1859 by the US Army, and between 1909 and 1912 served as a military prison. Barracks, casemates, the guardhouse, a chapel and parade ground linger from this period. Some of the later buildings used by the Federal Penitentiary staff are now in ruins, such as the Warden's

Burt Lancaster plays the Birdman of Alcatraz (1962)

House and Post Exchange (then used as a shop and sports hall). After the closure of the prison, the island was occupied between 1969 and 1971 by American Indians campaigning for native rights.

Fires and vandalism destroyed some buildings, and faded graffiti can still be seen in places. Since 1972 Alcatraz has been part of the Golden Gate National Recreation Area.

Exploring Alcatraz

The crossing to the island takes 15 minutes. Visitors can stay as long as the ferry schedules permit, but there are no refreshment or picnic facilities on the island. A Park Ranger greets each ferry and provides information. If you like to enjoy the island at your own pace a brochure with a self-guiding trail is available. There is also a useful 12-minute film on the history of the island screened in the dockside buildings, and Ranger-led tours on themes such as natural history, escape attempts and the native American presence.

Cellhouse

A 35-minute self-guided audio tour using the voices of former inmates and prison officers brings to life the cell blocks and living quarters. Corridors were given ironic nicknames like "Broadway," "Times Square" and "Seedy Street," and the violent activities of the 250 convicts provided rich material for the writers of headlines and film scripts. An exhibit in one cell shows how three of them, Frank Lee Morris and the Anglin brothers, attempted to escape by digging through their walls and leaving dummy heads in bed to fool prison staff. Visitors can also see the dining hall, recreation yard and prison gardens.

Ferry: Red & White from Pier 41. Tel: 415/546–2628. In summer first boat leaves 9:30am, last returns 6:30pm. Admission to

the island is free but there is a charge for the ferry and optional audio tour. Advance booking by credit card is strongly recommended to avoid a lengthy wait. Tel: 415/546–2700. Ranger Program Information – tel: 415/705–1042.

Once home to America's hardened criminals, the prison cells are now open to tourists

---

ESCAPE FROM ALCATRAZ

The 14 recorded escape attempts from Alcatraz range from the brutal to the ingenious. Some prisoners were shot dead by guards, others were found hiding on the island, and many were frustrated by the icy waters of the Bay. In 1945 John Giles, who worked in the prison laundry, reached San Francisco disguised in military uniform but was immediately recaptured. No prisoner is known to have got off the island alive, though five are still missing. On the last attempt in 1962 John Paul Scott managed to swim to rocks beside the Golden Gate Bridge, but was too exhausted to get further away.

The scenic location of Alcatraz Island belies the brutal history of its prison

The "Postcard Row" of Victorian mansions in Alamo Square is a landmark of city architecture

ALAMO SQUARE

A showcase for the city's Victorian mansions, this grassy hilltop offers one of the most photographed scenic views of the city. Steiner Street, on its east side, is a bright cascade of Queen Anne "painted ladies" (see pages 78–9), including a splendid buttermilk madam at no 850. Behind this "Postcard Row," in vivid contrast, soar the skyscraping tower blocks of the Financial District raised a century later.

Set aside as a park in 1856, this historic district developed quickly in the 1890s and has an appealing architectural unity. The neighborhood to the north is known as the Western Addition from the planned westward expansion of the city that took place in the last quarter of the 19th century. Settled by the Japanese and then African-American communities, many of its Victorian buildings were demolished in the 1960s and replaced by grim housing projects. *Bus: 21. Avoid the park at night.*

ANSEL ADAMS CENTER FOR PHOTOGRAPHY

The San Francisco-born photographer Ansel Adams (1902–84) is best known for his perceptive homages to the American landscape, and many Californians have a deep affection for his black-and-white portraits of Yosemite Valley taken in the 1930s. A selection of his work is always displayed in this gallery, which also stages stimulating exhibitions of contemporary photography. The bookstore has a good range of books devoted to Adams and the art of photography. *250 Fourth Street, on the southwest*

corner of Yerba Buena Gardens. Tel:
415/495–7000. Open: Tuesday to Sunday
11am–5pm (8pm first Thursday of the
month). Closed: Monday. Admission
charge. Metro: Powell. Bus: 30, 45, 76.

AQUATIC PARK

At the west end of Fisherman's Wharf,
this small beach and park was created in
the 1930s and is a microcosm of San
Francisco. Tourists come for its historic
ships, cable cars and the shops of
Ghirardelli Square, but you're also likely
to encounter crafts stalls, kite fliers,
paddling children, sand-sculpting
panhandlers and hippies chanting to the
sunset. Walk around its curling pier,
always popular with crab fishermen, to
look back at the city.
*Beach Street at Polk Street. Cable car:
Powell/Hyde. Bus: 19, 30, 42.*

ASIAN ART MUSEUM

The largest museum devoted to Asian art
outside that continent is filled for the
most part by the priceless collection of
the late millionaire Avery Brundage, a
long-serving president
of the International
Olympic Committee.
Its 12,000 treasures
cover 6,000 years of
Asian art gathered from
more than 40
countries, and include
bronzes, porcelain,
textiles, paintings,
netsuke and Indian
sculpture.

The museum's
restful displays are
spread over two floors
in purpose-built
galleries that avoid
overwhelming the

visitor. They commence invitingly with
the Treasure Wall, an exquisite précis of
what the collection has in store. The first
floor is devoted almost entirely to Chinese
art, including an amazing assembly of
jade works and the oldest known dated
Chinese Buddha, from AD338. Upstairs a
large Japanese collection is complemented
by works from southeast Asia. A program
of changing exhibitions, which might
cover anything from Tibetan *samdra*
(message boards) to Korean *pojagi*
(decorative wrapping cloths), helps bring
other treasures to view.

The museum is
currently housed
beside the M H
de Young
Memorial
Museum (see
page 70), but
intends to move
into the former San
Francisco Main
Library building in
the Civic Center
(see page 49).
*Hagiwara Tea
Garden Drive, Golden
Gate Park. Tel:
415/668–8921. Open:
Wednesday to Sunday
10am–5pm (8:45pm
first Wednesday of
month). Closed:
Monday, Tuesday.
Admission charge, but
free first Wednesday
and Saturday of month
10am–noon. Bus: 5,
21, 44.*

Ansel Adams Center
(left); Asian Art
Museum (above)

CABLE CAR BARN AND MUSEUM

An integral part of San Franciscan life and lore, cable cars have been running in the city since 1873 (see page 27). At the heart of the network is a redbrick building just west of Chinatown, where the singing cables wind round huge spinning drums. Built in 1909 as the Ferry and Cliffhouse Railways Powerhouse, the Cable Car Barn is still used as a maintenance and control center, but now also doubles as a working museum explaining the history and inner mysteries of this unique system.

Downstairs in the oily Sheave Room, a viewing area enables visitors to see the great drum wheels turning beneath the intersection of Mason and Washington Streets. Upstairs, a second viewing platform overlooks the beautiful spinning wheels powering the woven steel cables, which must have made a pretty picture of Victorian industry in the days of steam.

The cables have to be replaced at least once a year, a task carried out overnight.

The adjacent area is filled with several historic cable cars, including one from Hallidie's original 1873 fleet. Its survival is something of a miracle, as it was on loan for an exhibition in Baltimore when the 1906 earthquake struck San Francisco. The following year that city was struck by a great fire, but the car escaped damage and was subsequently discovered in 1939 lingering in a local junkyard. A shop sells books and souvenirs, while display panels and a video show tell the story of San Francisco's cable cars.

Washington Street at Mason Street. Tel: 415/474–1887. Open: daily 10am–6pm (5pm November to March). Free. Cable car: Powell/Mason, Powell/Hyde. Bus: 1.

Travels in time: a vintage car on display in the Cable Car Barn and Museum

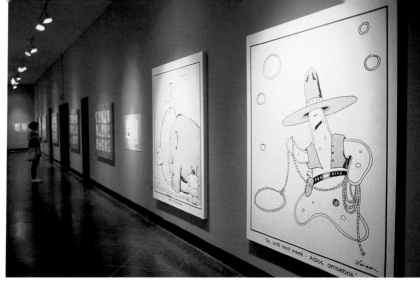
See the funny side of science in the cartoon gallery at the California Academy of Sciences

CALIFORNIA ACADEMY OF SCIENCES

Typical of the American passion for creating museums that can educate both adults and children in an unstupefying way, this science and natural history museum attracts 1.5 million visitors a year. Its buildings have evolved over the century and focus on the central Fountain Courtyard – the statue of *Mating Whales* is a relic from the 1939 World Fair on Treasure Island (see page 88). Some space is given over to traveling exhibitions, and there is a downstairs café and well-stocked bookstores and gift shops. The Discovery Room offers hands-on exploration for children and the disabled.

Natural History and Science Museums

A gallery to the right of the entrance foyer illustrates the wildlife of Wild California, with an adjacent Gem and Mineral Hall. On the opposite side the main galleries commence with a re-creation of the African savannah and its game. The Earth and Space Hall includes "Safequake," a trembling exhibit that simulates the feeling of an earthquake. Other halls include a survey of the diverse human cultures around the world, a gallery of science cartoons by Gary Larson, and "Life Through Time," which traces 3.5 billion years of evolution.

Morrison Planetarium

A celestial pleasure dome offering ethereal evocations of the night sky and laser shows with pounding soundtracks. *Call for times. Sky shows, tel: 415/750–7141. Laser shows, tel: 415/750–7138. Admission charge.*

Steinhart Aquarium

Behold the silent frenzy of the deep in the company of over a thousand species of freshwater and saltwater fish. *Music Concourse Drive, Golden Gate Park. Tel: 415/750–7145. Open: daily 10am–7pm (5pm winter). Admission charge, but free first Wednesday of the month. Bus: 5, 21, 44.*

California Palace of the Legion of Honor

CALIFORNIA PALACE OF THE LEGION OF HONOR

Prestigiously located in the northwest corner of Lincoln Park, this fine arts museum was built in 1924 by the sugar baron Adolph Spreckels and his wife Alma. It is dedicated to the Californians who fell in World War I, and was designed in Beaux-Arts style by George Applegarth as a replica of the Hôtel de Salm in Paris. It was there that Napoleon Bonaparte established the Légion d'Honneur, the premier military and civil order of merit in France.

The building reopened in 1995 after a substantial three-year renovation that included the addition of a skylit courtyard surrounded by six lower-level galleries where special exhibitions are held. There is also a theater, book store, restaurant and a café with views out to the Pacific Ocean.

The museum's permanent collection spans 4,000 years of ancient and European art from 2500BC to this century. As well as major masterpieces

by artists such as El Greco, Rembrandt, Watteau, Monet and Picasso. Exhibits range fgrom tapestries, costumes and porcelain to a rich tapestry of books, prints and drawings collected by the Achenbach Foundation for Graphic Arts. A key attraction is a collection of over 70 sculptures by Rodin – one of the several casts made of his famous bronze *Le Penseur* greets visitors arriving in the Palace's colonnaded front courtyard. *Lincoln Park, 34th Avenue and Clement Street. Tel: 415/750–3600. Open: Tuesday to Sunday 10am–5pm (8:45pm first Saturday of the month). Closed: Monday. Admission charge, but free second Wednesday of the month. Bus: 18, 38.*

CANNERY

The least gaudy of the shopping and entertainment complexes lining Fisherman's Wharf, the redbrick Cannery was built in 1907 and was once the largest fruit and vegetable canning

factory in the world. Today its warehouses and tree-lined courtyards are used to pack in tourists with the help of street performers, souvenir shops, clothes boutiques, art galleries and a please-everyone range of restaurants and cafés. Cobb's Comedy Club, a showcase for comedians, is located here (see page 145).

Museum of the City of San Francisco
An absorbing miscellany of San Franciscan memorabilia plus enthusiastic staff make this small museum worth seeking out. Some of its exhibits are commendably bizarre and monumental, such as the golden head from the 22-foot-high illuminated statue of the *Goddess of Progress* that capped City Hall prior to the 1906 earthquake, and a 13th-century carved wooden ceiling that

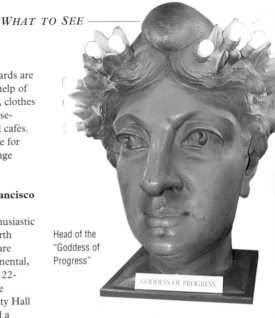

Head of the "Goddess of Progress"

GODDESS OF PROGRESS

The Cannery: one of the best of San Francisco's many shopping and dining complexes

the publisher William Randolph Hearst had shipped over from a palace in Spain.

Other finds reflect the human details of city life – crockery fused together by the heat of the 1906 post-earthquake conflagration, atmospheric old photographs of Chinatown, a commemorative souvenir bearing the lyrics of "I Left My Heart in San Francisco" and transcript conversations from emergency calls made by the public immediately after the 1989 Loma Prieta earthquake. A coin-fed piano from 1913 pumps out jolly rag-time tunes, ensuring that a good time is had by all.
Third floor, The Cannery. Tel: 415/928–0289. Open: Wednesday to Sunday 10am–4pm. Closed: Monday, Tuesday. Donations welcome.

The Cannery, 2801 Leavenworth Street at Beach Street. Tel: 415/771–3112. Free. Cable car: Powell/Hyde. Bus: 32.

CARTOON ART MUSEUM

Constantly popping up in newspapers, magazines, ads and animated films, cartoon art is a brash and colorful squatter in the palace of American culture. This museum has a permanent collection of around 10,000 examples dating from the 1730s, and regularly mounts exhibitions. Close to Yerba Buena Gardens, its facilities include an interactive CD-ROM gallery, children's museum and bookstore.

Cartoons will never be the same once you have visited the Cartoon Art Museum

814 Mission Street, Suite 200 (near 4th Street). Tel: 415/546–3922. Open: Wednesday to Friday 11am–5pm, Saturday 10am–5pm, Sunday 1–5pm. Closed: Monday, Tuesday. Admission charge. Metro: Powell. Bus: 12, 14, 30.

CASTRO

Whatever your sexuality, San Francisco's world-famous gay neighborhood is worth seeing (see pages 44–5). Contrary to the reservations of many tourists, it is safe and welcoming to both men and women and a fun place to shop, drink and spend time. While there are a few seedy bars, as there are in all parts of the city, the neighborhood is a flourishing tribute to the "pink economy" and the warmth and humur of its residents.

The best introduction to the history and achievements of the Castro is to take a guided walking tour (see page 30). Two blocks in Castro Street, from Market Street south to 19th Street, form its core, and are signposted by the 1924 Castro Theater – a classic old-style movie palace complete with ascending Wurlitzer organ. Though its shops and bars come and go, several have become neighborhood landmarks, such as Cliff's Variety hardware store, a heaven for homebuilders and dresskmakers, and the gay and lesbian bookstore, A Different Light. On the eastern corner with Market Street, the Twin Peaks Bar pioneered the coming out of the Castro by having large picture windows and an openly gay clientele for all the world to admire.

Names Project

On the northeast corner of the Castro and Market Streets intersection, this is the center of the worldwide AIDS Memorial Quilt network. Continuing in the American tradition of sewing bees and quilt-making, this San Francisco-born project encourages the making and display of textile panels honoring the victims of AIDS.

Friends and partners have been creating these since 1987 – each panel measures three feet by six feet and includes personal mementoes ranging from photographs and hand-painted messages to locks of hair, car keys and

Barbie dolls. The panels are then sewn together in sets of eight and publicly displayed around the country and abroad. To date some 30,000 have been made, representing about 12 percent of AIDS deaths in the US. Panels also come from similar projects in many other countries.

The Project has sewing machines, fabrics and materials available for quilt-makers to use, and there are always several completed examples on display. Their inventive, colorful and celebratory designs provide a deeply moving record of the men and women caught up in the AIDS epidemic. An adjacent shop sells gifts with proceeds going to related causes.
2362 Market Street. Tel: 415/863–1966. Open: daily noon–5pm. Free. Metro: Castro Street. Bus: 8, 24, 33.

CENTER FOR THE ARTS

Opened in 1993 as part of the Yerba Buena Gardens development (see page 91), this multi-million dollar arts center combines art galleries, film and performance theaters, a gift shop and the OPTS Café. A major venue for traveling exhibitions and performers, its cultural agenda reflects a commitment to promoting Bay Area artists and the diversity of its communities.
701 Mission Street at Third Street. Tel: 415/978–2787. Galleries open: Tuesday to Sunday 11am–6pm (8pm Thursday). Closed: Monday. Admission charge but free 6pm–8pm first Thursday of the month. Metro: Montgomery. Bus: 14, 15, 30, 45.

The 1924 Castro Cinema marks the gateway to San Francisco's gay neighborhood

GLAD TO BE GAY

San Francisco's gay and lesbian community came to the fore in the 1970s and is now firmly established in the mainstream of its life. The city's reputation as a gay haven emerged during World War II, when the US military systematically expelled homosexuals from their ranks – for those serving in the Pacific arena, that meant the port of San Francisco. Rather than go home to hostility, the servicemen formed their own enclaves here.

Castro stars (left); gay and lesbian flag (right); Freedom Day Parade (above and bottom right)

A second gay immigration followed during the McCarthy era, when homosexuals were purged from government positions. In the 1960s antagonism by the police and the wooing of the gay vote by liberal politicians brought gay rights issues into the open. As the hippy revolution endorsed more liberated lifestyles, San Franciscan gays drifted from Haight-Ashbury into the cheap housing of the adjacent Castro district.

Today the Castro is the archetypal gay neighborhood (see page 42), though what might have been a storybook evolution from ghetto to mecca has been marred by two tragedies that have ultimately proved catalytic rallying points. The first was the murder of the openly homosexual politician Harvey Milk, who was elected a city Supervisor

in 1977. He was gunned down on November 28, 1978, by Dan White, a disaffected former policeman who became infuriated by Milk's liberal policies. White's trial provoked angry demonstrations, and now Harvey Milk has joined the pantheon of martyred American political heroes.

In 1981 AIDS surfaced, cooling the party atmosphere in the Castro and causing devastating losses by the mid-1980s. San Francisco's gays and lesbians have been at the forefront of the response to this worldwide epidemic, including the creation of memorial quilts known as the Names Project (see pages 42–3).

Gay and lesbian life in San Francisco is no longer confined to the Castro – Valencia Street in the Mission, for example, has a large number of lesbian and feminist stores and meeting places. Conversely, celebrations such as Halloween, the Freedom Day Parade, and Gay Pride Week now attract many straight San Franciscans to the Castro.

Chinatown

Most of the Chinese who have settled in America trace their roots back to Guandong province, an area on the coast of southeast China of similar size to the Bay Area. Many came initially as unskilled labor, working in the Gold Rush mines, as farmworkers, and providing 90 percent of the workforce that constructed the Central Pacific Railroad. San Francisco was their port of arrival, and it was here that they established their largest enclave. By 1880 Chinatown had 21,000 inhabitants, though only a thousand of these were women.

The fires ignited by the 1906 earthquake not only destroyed the old Chinatown but its immigration records too, enabling many Chinese to claim American citizenship and bring their children across the Pacific. The community backed the 1911 revolution against the Manchu dynasty and the Nationalist cause in the long-running feud with mainland Communist China. Today San Francisco's Chinese-American community is spread far beyond Chinatown – a second enclave has emerged around Clement Street in the Richmond district, and there is another Chinatown in Oakland.

Grant Avenue

The entrance gate to Chinatown is at the south end of Grant Avenue at Bush Street. Grant Avenue is the neighborhood's high street, packed with shops and restaurants with bright façades that attract both tourists and residents. See pages 94–5 for a walking tour.

Bank of Canton

Nothing brings home the complexity of Chinatown better than the story of the Chinatown Telephone Exchange. This vivid, pagoda-roofed building, which now belongs to the Bank of Canton, was constructed in 1909 and was the first

post-earthquake building to be demonstratively Chinese in appearance.

Designed like a temple, it housed a unique foreign-language telephone exchange that required operators to not only speak English and five Chinese dialects but also memorize 2,100 residents' names and their phone numbers. When a long-distance call came in, a runner would be sent dashing down the alleys – a pool of male and female messengers were kept on stand-by and fired off according to the sex of the recipient. The Exchange closed in 1949 when the duller world of automation arrived.
743 Washington Street.

Chinese Culture Center

This small exhibition space and shop in the Holiday Inn Hotel puts on changing shows relevant to the Chinese-American heritage. It also arranges historical and culinary tours of Chinatown.
750 Kearny Street, Third Floor. Tel: 415/986–1822. Open: Tuesday to Saturday 10am–4pm; Sunday noon–4pm. Closed: Monday. Free.

Chinese Historical Society

This one-room basement offers a highly informative crash course in the history of the Chinese community in San Francisco and America. It is a gripping story that starts in the exploited days of the coolie trade, moves to the racist hostility and exclusionary immigration laws of the 1880s, rides out the 1906 earthquake, then progresses through the "gilded ghetto" days of post-war Chinatown to the open and accepted society of today. *650 Commercial Street. Tel: 415/391–1188. Open: Tuesday to Saturday noon–4pm. Closed: Sunday, Monday. Donations appreciated.*

Old St Mary's Church
See page 94.

Portsmouth Square
See pages 80–1.
Cable car: California Street. Bus: 1, 15, 30, 45.

DIM-SUM
There is no better introduction to the immense variety of flavors and textures in Cantonese food than a *dim-sum* meal. Served from mid-morning to mid-afternoon, this is a refreshingly menu-free experience. Diners choose from a passing trolley laden with sweet and savory Chinese delicacies – dumplings stuffed with meat and fish, spring rolls, deep-fried dishes, steamed buns and the elaborate specialities of the house. Bills are calculated by the number of saucers you pile up.

Always busy, the streets of Chinatown are lined with brightly colored lights and signs

Civic Center

*T*he official heart, public smile and open arms (but not the soul) of San Francisco are contained within its Civic Center. Sitting in the triangle formed by the arteries of Van Ness Avenue and Market Street, this assembly of administrative offices, arts venues and public spaces reflects the civic zeal that erupted after the 1906 earthquake.

City Hall

Designed by Arthur Brown Jr and John Bakewell Jr in 1915, City Hall epitomizes the vogue for the Beaux-Arts style rampant at that time. Both architects had been students of the influential École des Beaux-Arts in Paris, which sang the virtues of the colossal, the symmetrical and the classical. Its baroque dome is modeled on St Peter's in Rome, and the parade of allegorical sculpture on the pediment above the Polk Street entrance is by the French artist Henri Crenier. Its figures depict high-minded notions like

Shoppers at the twice-weekly Heart of the City Farmers' Market in United Nations Plaza

the Wealth of California, Trade and Navigation. Round the back, the relentless traffic on Van Ness Avenue appears to have little time for Wisdom, Learning and Truth.
400 Van Ness Avenue. The building is closed for seismic re-fit (due to open 1998).

Civic Center Plaza

This tree-lined plaza in front of City Hall sometimes becomes an animated protest arena, but for much of the year it serves as an open-air dormitory for the homeless. Begging can be a problem at times, so visitors should exercise caution as well as charity. Underneath the plaza is Brooks Hall, a conference center, and

on the south side the 1915 Bill Graham
Civic Auditorium, named in honor of the
rock music impresario. On the north side
is the 1926 Old State Building and,
under construction, a new Court House.

West of Van Ness Avenue
Built parallel with City Hall are the War
Memorial Opera House and the
Veterans' Building, both completed in
1932 and dedicated to the soldiers of
World War I. To their north is the 1986
New State Building, prominently
displaying the Seal of California. South
of the opera house is the 1980 Louise M
Davies Symphony Hall.

San Francisco Main Library
Built in 1917, this public library has the
small Museum of the City of San
Francisco on its third floor. Its
miscellaneous collection of historic finds
includes souvenirs from the Panama–
Pacific International Exposition and
various gifts to the city, such as a bronze
bear donated by the citizens of Berlin in
1969. Its computer files include an
archive of historic photos of the city and
a CD-ROM showing a jerky film taken in
1905 from a cable car traveling down
Market Street. In order to suggest San
Francisco was a great city of automobiles,
several cars drive repeatedly in front of
the camera – one as many as 10 times.

The library and museum is scheduled
to relocate to a new building opposite,
designed by I M Pei. The vacated space
will be taken over by the Museum of
Asian Art currently in Golden Gate Park.
Between the two libraries is the 1894
Lick Monument, depicting Californian
heroes.
_Larkin and McAllister Streets. Tel:
415/557–4400. Library open: Monday,
Wednesday, Thursday, Saturday_

EARLY DAYS

Christianity comes to the Indian – imperious
figures on the Lick Monument, Civic Center

_10am–6pm; Tuesday, Friday noon–6pm.
Closed: Tuesday and Friday mornings,
Sunday. Museum open: Tuesday to Friday
1–6pm plus Thursday and Saturday
10am–noon. Closed: Sunday, Monday plus
Tuesday, Wednesday, Friday mornings. Free._

United Nations Plaza
East of Hyde Street stands the Federal
Building, and beside it the United
Nations Plaza with an equestrian statue of
Simón Bolívar, the liberator of South
America. The name of the plaza
commemorates the signing of the UN
Charter in 1945 in the nearby War
Memorial Opera House. The Heart of the
City Farmers' Market takes place here
every Wednesday and Sunday.
_Polk and McAllister Streets. Metro: Civic
Center. Bus: 5, 21._

Today's Cliff House (above) and the seaside palace built by Adolf Sutro in 1896 (right)

CLIFF HOUSE

Perched on the headlands of Point Lobos, with the windswept runway of Ocean Beach stretching southward, Cliff House is where San Francisco conducts its long-running romance with the seaside. The leading protagonist is Adolph Sutro, a philanthropic German immigrant who made a fortune from building a drainage tunnel for the Comstock silver mines in the 1870s and then became a property developer and San Francisco mayor. He and his family lived just across Great Highway in what is now Sutro Heights Park (see page 133).

The present Cliff House, dating from 1909, is but a faint shadow of the grand, eight-storey mock-château Sutro built on the site in 1896. This ornate Victorian palace, with its dining rooms, dance floors and observation tower, formed the flamboyant centerpiece in a bathing resort that included the Sutro Baths and a railway line to bring daytrippers from the city. That building burnt down in 1907, but is well remembered in the many photographs displayed around today's Cliff House. This is now part of the Golden Gate National Recreation Area. Steps lead down to a Visitor Center where you can learn more about the resort's history and its marine life. Other attractions are a Camera Obscura and the Musée Mecanique, an arcade full of

historic amusements. Inside the Cliff House is a restaurant and bar.
Visitor Center – tel: 415/556–8642. Open: daily 10am–5pm. Admission charge for Camera Obscura.

Point Lobos

The Spanish named this part of the coast after the barking *lobos marinos* (sea wolves) they found living among its rocks and waters. Sea-lions still cavort around the guano-iced Seal Rocks off Cliff House, where you can also see a variety of seabirds including black cormorants, brown pelicans and gulls.

Sutro Baths

Covering three acres to the north of Cliff House, the ruins of the world's largest bathhouse make a poignant sight among the rocks. Opened in 1886, the Sutro Baths once accommodated 24,000 swimmers in six variable temperature saltwater and freshwater pools. The number of visitors gradually drained away after World War I and the baths were turned into an ice rink, then burnt down in 1966.

Cliff House, 1066–1090 Point Lobos Avenue. Bus: 38, 38L.

COIT TOWER

See page 86.

EMBARCADERO

Curving round the city's northeastern corner from China Basin to Fisherman's Wharf, this six-mile waterfront illustrates San Francisco's gradual transition from thriving port to international leisure center. At its center stands the landmark Ferry Building, commandingly sited at the end of Market Street. Built in 1903, its clock tower was modeled on the Giralda in Seville. Though it still functions as a ferry terminus, there is little to remind us of the great city gateway through which 50 million passengers once poured annually – a stream stemmed by the opening of the Bay and Golden Gate Bridges.

North of the Ferry Building, the Embarcadero's piers bear odd numbers. Pier 7 has been converted into a restful riverwalk and others now house offices and studios, but cruise liners still dock at Pier 35. To the south, beyond the Bay Bridge, the piers have even numbers. Known as South Beach, this area is now gentrifying with new apartments, restaurants and a palm tree-lined walkway.

Ruins of the Sutro Baths, once furnished with stained glass and classical sculptures

EXPLORATORIUM

Imagine a mad scientist's workshop invaded by a school trip, and you have the rough-and-ready, hands-on, kid-friendly, back-of-the-garage world of the Exploratorium. Running behind the Palace of Fine Arts (see pages 76–7), this hangar-like laboratory rejoices in the mysteries of natural phenomena, then sets you working it all out with all necessary tools provided. If it's raining and the kids are looking glum, this is your salvation.

Built on two floors, the Exploratorium is loosely divided into areas exploring subjects like Resonance, Weather and Electricity, with plenty of exhorting commands like "Create a Mini-Tornado!" and "Sing into Vidium!" beside the exhibits. The result is baffling and enjoyable entertainment for both children and adults, backed up by a gift store and very necessary café. Many of the most fascinating interactions are designed by artists-in-residence, like the pop video-style Recollections by Ed Tannebaum. The most popular exhibit is the Tactile Dome, a completely dark crawl-round geodesic dome which you explore through touch, and which requires prior reservation.

3601 Lyon Street at Marina Boulevard. Tel: 415/563–7337. Tactile Dome reservations – tel: 415/561–0362 (over-sevens only). Open: daily in summer 10am–5pm (9:30pm Wednesday), rest of year Tuesday to Sunday. Closed: Monday (except summer). Admission charge, but free first Wednesday of the month. Bus: 30.

FINANCIAL DISTRICT

Strolling between skyscrapers is one of the particular joys of America's great cities, and San Francisco's compact but extremely elevated Financial District presents a classic mix of historic and contemporary big money architecture (see pages 92–3).

The city's tallest building is the 853-foot Transamerica Pyramid (see page 87), closely followed by the 779-foot carnelian-clad Bank of America World Headquarters (555 California Street) and the 724-foot First Interstate Center (345 California Street), where the top 11 floors are occupied by the luxury Mandarin Oriental Hotel. Much of the eastern corner of the Financial District is given over to the eight-block Embarcadero Center, which combines shops, restaurants, offices and the Hyatt

The Transamerica Pyramid – a beacon amid the skyscrapers of the Financial District

Pier group: ferry trips, Bay cruises and Alcatraz tours depart from Fisherman's Wharf

Regency Hotel. The latter is crowned by a revolving restaurant where you can enjoy a leisurely overview of these pillars of money.

In the triangle formed by Kearny, Market and Washington streets. Cable car: California Street. Metro: Montgomery. Bus: 1, 15, 42.

FISHERMAN'S WHARF

Fisherman's Wharf is the city's most visited attraction, which is a pity as it has little to do with the real and memorable San Francisco. Its frenzied parade of low-rise hotels, shopping centers, souvenir shops, seafood stalls and waterfront restaurants runs east from Aquatic Park to the climactic consumer gore of Pier 39 (see page 77). Providing you forestall disappointment by going in

the full knowledge that it is shamelessly devoted to tourist-wooing commerce, you will emerge poorer but mentally unscathed.

In the 1860s there was just a beach here (now Beach Street), but by the start of this century so many Genoese and Sicilian boats were moored here the area was known as "Italy Harbor." Its days as a hard-working wharf are all but over, but an air of salty realism lingers down unfragrant walkways like Fish Alley and Pier 47, and beside Jefferson Lagoon where the sports fishing boats tie up. Ferries to Alcatraz and Sausalito leave from Pier 41. See also relevant entries for Hyde Street Pier, the Cannery and USS *Pampanito*.

Jefferson Street. Cable car: Powell/Hyde, Powell/Mason. Bus: 32, 42.

EARTHQUAKE

"**E**verybody was gracious. The most perfect courtesy obtained. Never, in all San Francisco's history, were her people so kind and courteous as on this night of terror." Thus Jack London described the aftermath of the earthquake of April 18, 1906, the worst in American history.

Estimated at 8.3 on the Richter Scale, the 1906 'quake lasted for less than a minute but led to the devastation of much of the city. Hampered by burst water mains and collapsed buildings, fire crews were unable to contain the ensuing blazes that ravaged the city for three days. Some 3,000 citizens are thought to have died, and a great stretch of the city's northeast corner was reduced to rubble.

1906: havoc in the streets (below) and widespread fire damage (right)

1989: fires in the Marina district (left) and a collapsed road on the Bay Bridge (below)

Within six years San Francisco had been rebuilt, but the memory of this cataclysm lingers in its psyche. Every resident knows it could happen again, any time, and few visitors leave without wondering if it's living on the fault line that puts the zing in this audacious city.

On October 17, 1989, it did happen again – scoring 7.1 this time and causing over 60 deaths in the Bay Area. Known as "Loma Prieta" from its epicenter near Santa Cruz, the earthquake brought down a section of the Bay Bridge and buildings in the Marina, and provoked the demolition of the waterfront Embarcadero freeway – now considered a blessing.

San Franciscans remain phlegmatic about this ever-imminent catastrophe. Loma Prieta inspired black-humored souvenirs like wobbly mugs and Richter Scale Ale, and visitors to the California Academy of Sciences still line up to experience its simulated earthquake machine.

Buildings close for "seismic retrofit", office-workers conduct earthquake drills, shops advise worried tourists to hide under the table – but all San Franciscans know that the only worthwhile safety measure is to get as much happiness and partying under your belt while you can. They understand that the planet is a-rippling and a-rumbling all the time, so don't be surprised if you're driving down the freeway and the soft-spoken DJ on the radio prefaces the next Jefferson Airplane track with a nonchalant announcement that "Mother Earth has just had another of her little tremors."

Fort Mason Center

*O*ccupying a prime location on the city's northernmost promontory, the buildings and grounds of Fort Mason exemplify the San Franciscans' laudable knack for turning former military posts into bases for cultural activity. Originally fortified by the Spanish in 1797, the site was taken over by squatters in the Gold Rush, then made into a US Army post during the Civil War. Its busiest hour came in World War II when 1.5 million troops passed through en route to the Pacific war zones. In 1962 its military duties transferred to Oakland, and since 1977 it has been part of the Golden Gate National Recreation Area.

Crafty looks: masks are among many colorful goods on sale at the Mexican Museum gift shop

The Fort Mason Center now inhabits its waterside piers and wooden warehouses, while other historic buildings are used by the GGNRA and military personnel. As well as specialist museums and theaters, the acclaimed vegetarian restaurant Greens (see page 166), which looks on to the Bay, makes a trip here worthwhile.

Museo Italo-Americano
The museum seeks to preserve the heritage of Italian-Americans by staging exhibitions of Italian art and culture and work by Italian-American artists.
Building C. Tel: 415/673–2200. Open: Wednesday to Sunday noon–5pm. Closed: Monday, Tuesday. Admission charge.

Mexican Museum
Dedicated to Mexican and Mexican-American culture, this museum presents exhibitions drawn from its own permanent collection and from the art of Latin America. Its gift store has a notable selection of Mexican textiles, tin mirrors, masks and other aesthetic crafts. The museum plans to move to a new location in Yerba Buena Gardens by 1998.
Building D. Tel: 415/441–0404. Open: Wednesday to Sunday noon–5pm. Closed: Monday, Tuesday and between exhibitions. Admission charge, but free first Wednesday of the month and open until 8pm.

San Francisco Craft and Folk Art Museum
Exhibitions of crafts from any source of interest and quality, including American folk art, traditional ethnic designs and contemporary Bay Area artists.
Building A. Tel: 415/775-0990. Open: Tuesday to Sunday 11am–5pm (10am Saturday). Closed: Monday. Admission charge, but free first Wednesday of the month and open to 8pm.

Once occupied by the military, the buildings of Fort Mason are now used for cultural activities

San Francisco African-American Historical and Cultural Society

A small museum devoted to the history and culture of African-Americans, with an exhibition gallery, resource center and gift store.

Building C, Room 165. Tel: 415/441–0640. Open: Wednesday to Sunday noon–5pm. Closed: Monday, Tuesday. Admission charge, but first Wednesday of the month free and open to 8pm.

SS *Jeremiah O'Brien*

This is the last unaltered example of the 2,700 Liberty ships built at great speed to carry cargo in World War II. The spartan SS *Jeremiah O'Brien* was constructed in Maine in 1943 in just 57 days and made several transatlantic crossings in the run-up to D-Day. A recent commemorative trip to join the 50th anniversary celebrations of the Allied invasion proved that the ship remains fighting fit.

Pier 3 East. Tel: 415/441–3101. Open: daily 9am–3pm (4pm weekends). Bay cruises in May. Admission charge.

Fort Mason Center – tel: 415/979–3010. Main entrance at Marina Boulevard by Buchanan Street. Bus: 28. Walkers can also follow Golden Gate Promenade west from Aquatic Park.

WORLD WAR II

The Japanese attack on Hawaii on December 7, 1941, had a long-lasting effect on San Francisco. The port became the chief embarkation point for the war in the Pacific, its coastal headlands were fortified against invasion, and naval shipbuilding yards were constructed at Sausalito and Richmond. While Japanese-Americans were being arrested and interned, African-American civilians arrived to work in the docks and factories, settling in neighborhoods such as Hunter's Point and the Western Addition. At the end of the war in 1945 many soldiers and workers stayed on, transforming the social matrix of the city forever.

Big guns: built by the military to protect the Golden Gate, Fort Point is now a historic site

FORT POINT NATIONAL HISTORIC SITE

Tucked under the carcass of Golden Gate Bridge, Fort Point was constructed between 1853 and 1861 to defend the city and Bay, but has never fired a shot in anger. It must have been a bleak posting, judging by the memoirs of one lighthouse keeper who recorded in 1915 that "there is the ocean and the sand and the guns and the soldiers. That is all. It grows monotonous."

Fort Point is still as chilly as ever, but there is a satisfaction in its functional military architecture, weathered brickwork, and the arsenal of historic cannon and guns displayed within its massive walls. Amongst these is a bronze cannon of 1684 that has miraculously survived from the original adobe castillo built here by the Spanish in 1794. A museum displays military uniforms, equipment, photographs and menus suggesting that the early 19th-century US soldier ate an awful lot of meat hash and Irish stew. Other exhibits trace the contribution of women to military life and the four-year construction of the Golden Gate Bridge.

Fort Point is part of the Golden Gate National Recreation Area and has a Visitor Center by the entrance. Exhibitions of cannon-firing and drill in Civil War uniform are held regularly – call for times. See page 104 for cycle ride. *Tel: 415/556–1693. Open: Wednesday to Sunday 10am–5pm. Closed: Monday, Tuesday. Free. Bus: 28, 29.*

GHIRARDELLI SQUARE

Behind this much-publicized chocolate factory and shopping center on the south side of Aquatic Park lies a classic San Franciscan tale of the Gold Rush immigrant made good. The Italian-born Domingo Ghirardelli arrived in the city in 1849 at the age of 32 to seek his fortune. Failing to strike it rich by prospecting, he resorted to the family trade of chocolate-making, setting up his first factory in 1852. In 1895 the business moved to the former woollen mills that have now become Ghirardelli Square. Today most of the company's confectionery is made elsewhere, but the historic machinery can be seen in sweet action in the Ghirardelli Chocolate Manufactory and Soda Fountain – a chocoholics' heaven that oozes with hot fudge, ice-cream and sensual whirlpools of dark chocolate sauce.

Many of the other buildings on this redbrick manufacturing complex date from the start of the century and originally produced cocoa, mustard and blankets. Among the 55 shops and six eateries that now fill their levels, the seafood restaurant McCormick & Kuleto's and the quality Mandarin Chinese restaurant both enjoy fine views over the Bay.
900 North Point Street at Larkin Street. Tel: 415/775–5500. Cable car: Powell/Hyde. Bus: 19, 30, 42.

GOLDEN GATE BRIDGE

Opened in 1937, the Golden Gate Bridge is one of the greatest in the world (see pages 108–9). Many visitors assume its name derives from its shape and burning color, but the strait between San Francisco and the Marin Headlands has been known as the Golden Gate since 1846. It was so christened by an exploring US army officer, John C Frémont, in a respectful reference to the Golden Horn beside which Byzantium (now Istanbul) stood.

Used daily by an average 100,000 vehicles, the six-lane bridge has a line of toll booths on its south side where drivers coming into the city must pay for the privilege. There are vista points and parking at both ends facing the Bay side, and a main gift shop by Toll Plaza. You can walk across on either side, an epiphanic rite of passage that takes a good hour return – remember that it's cold and windy out there. (See page 104 for cycle ride.)
Highway 101. Bus: 28, 29, and 76 on Sunday only; Golden Gate Transit.

The shops of Ghirardelli Square are a must for souvenir-hunters and chocolate lovers

Golden Gate Park

A triumph of enlightened urban planning and visionary landscape gardening, the 1,017 acres of Golden Gate Park stretch for over three miles from Stanyan Street west to Ocean Beach. Besides being a green lung with walks and gardens, the park has three popular city museums – the California Academy of Sciences, the Asian Art Museum and the M H de Young Memorial Museum (see individual entries). Cultural sights include a Japanese tea garden, musical concourse, windmills, historic statues and even a Buffalo Paddock. Leisure activities include boating, horseriding, tennis and golf, and a children's playground with a restored 1912 carousel (see pages 98–9).

Open: daily 9am–5pm. Admission charge. Bus: 5, 21.

Japanese Tea Garden

Built for the 1894 Midwinter International Exposition, these harmonious gardens are a dainty world of crooked paths, poetic bridges, meditative pools, blazing pagodas and a lush variety of plants and trees. A teahouse serves Japanese and Chinese teas, and it is easy to imagine visitors in top hats and parasols enjoying the gardens a century ago.
Hagiwara Tea Garden Drive. Tel:

White hothouse: escape the turmoil of the city by visiting the Conservatory of Flowers

Conservatory of Flowers

Inspired by London's Kew Gardens, the conservatory was shipped over from Ireland in 1875 for the home of the millionaire James Lick. After his death it was erected in the park and is now a resplendent Victorian greenhouse with lily-clad fish ponds, orchids, ferns, tropical trees and bespectacled watercolorists.
In the northeast corner of the park by John F Kennedy Drive. Tel: 415/641–7978.

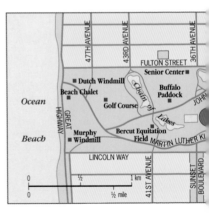

Visitors to the park have been enjoying its Japanese Tea Garden for over a century

415/752–1171. Open: daily 9am–6:30pm from March to September, 8:30am–6pm rest of year. Admission charge. Bus: 44.

Strybing Aboretum

Plants, trees and shrubs are laid out in geographical pockets from around the world, including a Garden of Native Californian Plants, redwood trees, and flora from South Africa, Australasia and Central America.

Junction of Hagiwara Tea Garden Drive and Martin Luther King Jr Drive. Tel: 415/661–1316. Open: Monday to Friday 8am–4:30pm, weekends 10am–5pm. Free. Bus: 44.

GOLDEN GATE PARK

BALBOA STREET
RICHMOND
CABRILLO STREET
TURK STREET

25TH AVENUE
PARK PRESIDIO BOULEVARD
10TH AVENUE
8TH AVENUE
6TH AVENUE
ARGUELLO BLVD

FULTON STREET
FULTON STREET

Spreckels Lake
Prayerbook Cross ①
Rose Garden
JOHN F KENNEDY DRIVE
Conservatory of Flowers
McLaren Lodge
FELL STREET

NNEDY DRIVE
Portals of the Past
Asian Art Museum
MH de Young Memorial Mus

Golden Gate Park Stadium & Polo Field
Stow Lake
Japanese Tea Garden
Music Concourse
John McLaren
Rhododendron Dell
OAK STREET

Strawberry Hill
KING JUNIOR
Morrison Planetarium
Steinhart Aquarium
California Academy of Sciences

Metson Lake
Elk Glen Lake
MARTIN LUTHER
Strybing Arboretum & Botanical Gardens
Shakespeare's Garden of Flowers
Kezar Stadium
WALLER ST
Kezar Pavilion

NIOR DRIVE
Mallard Lake
DRIVE
Hall of Flowers
FREDERICK ST

LINCOLN WAY
SUNSET
IRVING
STREET
LINCOLN WAY

25TH AVENUE
19TH AVENUE
14TH AVENUE
9TH AVENUE
7TH AVENUE
3RD AVENUE

Bronze door (right) of Grace Cathedral (above)

GRACE CATHEDRAL

Set atop Nob Hill, this modern replica of
the Notre-Dame cathedral in Paris was
designed by Lewis P Hobbart. Work
began in 1927 but the building was not
substantially finished until 1964. The
doors of its main façade are copies of the
famous Gates of Paradise designed by
Ghiberti in 1424 for the Baptistery in
Florence. The success of a recent appeal
has brought seismic reinforcements, a
monumental staircase up to the main
entrance, and a new chapter house on
Sacramento Street.

Despite its modernity, the church has
a remarkable and enveloping spirituality.
It is valued both as an official platform
where respected leaders such as Martin
Luther King Jr and Archbishop
Desmond Tutu have preached, and as a
force in the community – there are not
many cathedrals in the world that have a
basketball court underneath. A
permanent display pays respect to the
city's AIDS victims with quilts from the
Names Project (see pages 42–3).
*1051 Taylor Street at California Street. Tel:
415/776–6611. Open: daily, but access
restricted during services. Free. Cable car:
California. Bus: 1.*

HAAS-LILIENTHAL HOUSE

Exemplary of the Queen Anne style that
dominated San Francisco's Victorian
housing in the 1890s (see page 78), this
imposing mansion is the headquarters of
the Foundation for San Francisco's
Architectural Heritage, whose members
provide guided tours. It was built in
1886 for a German-born immigrant,

William Haas, who had a prosperous grocery business. The building was used as a family home by his heirs until 1972.

While the house doesn't quite live up to Gelette Burgess's critical view that the ideal Queen Anne "should be a restless, uncertain, frightful collection of details, giving the effect of a nightmare about to explode," it does bring home the haughty, cloistered lifestyle of the city's aspiring upper middle classes at that time. A basement museum provides books and information on the city's architectural heritage.

2007 Franklin Street. Tel: 415/441–3004. Open: Wednesday noon–3.15pm, Sunday 11am–4pm. Closed: Monday, Tuesday, Thursday to Saturday. Admission charge. Bus: 1, 12.

HAIGHT-ASHBURY

In the late 1960s San Francisco hosted one of the great spontaneous social experiments of our century, the hippy revolution (see page 64). Its epicenter was Haight-Ashbury, a Victorian neighborhood on the east side of Golden Gate Park that still clings to its counter-cultural roots and has the crazy streetlife to prove it. The best way to discover its haunts and history is to join a walking tour (see page 30); life gets wilder as the day goes on, so you may prefer to visit in the morning.

The core blocks of interest lie on Haight Street between Lyon and Stanyan Streets. While some of the Victorian mansions have been so smartened up it's hard to imagine they were once squats and crash-pads for Hell's Angels and drug-high rock singers, there are still enough shops selling tie-dye clothes, chimes, Afghan imports and anarchist tracts to keep the joss-stick of hippy heritage burning. Notable landmarks include the restaurant Dish (1398 Haight Street), once the infamous, marijuana-hazy Drogstore Café, the Haight-Ashbury Free Medical Clinic (558 Clayton Street), opened in 1967 and still dispensing free health care, and the hippy-revival Red Victorian Inn (1665 Haight Street).

To the south lies the steep and wooded Buena Vista Park, to the north the green strip of the Panhandle, originally designed as a carriage entrance to Golden Gate Park. The area also has a second flowering, known as the Lower Haight, further east by the junction with Fillmore Street.

Bus: 6, 7, 43, 71.

The Haight-Ashbury Free Medical Clinic has become a neighborhood institution

FLOWER POWER

"If you're going to San Francisco," Scott McKenzie sang in 1967, "be sure to wear some flowers in your hair." In that year the Haight-Ashbury district became a psychedelic back-drop for the finest hours of the hippy movement, when the Bay Area's alternative clans massed for a "Human Be-In" in Golden Gate Park and 500,000 flower children hit the city for the "Summer of Love."

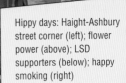

Hippy days: Haight-Ashbury street corner (left); flower power (above); LSD supporters (below); happy smoking (right)

"Hip" is thought to derive from Negro slang meaning "to be informed." The tuned in and turned on hippies shared the anti-establishment imperatives of their predecessors from North Beach, the Beat Generation, but took a more cosmic approach. Drugs, in particular LSD ("acid"), fueled their search for a new awareness, which was supplemented by a passionate

was but a brief, golden trip. By the autumn of 1967 violence and drug addiction were souring the dream, and "Hashbury" (as it was quickly dubbed) became a magnet for unsavory characters like the mass murderer Charles Manson. In October a "Death of the Hippie" march was staged, and the tourist buses went elsewhere.

Today the Haight is gentrifying, and nostalgia for that hippy dawn thrives. Its greatest achievement was probably its music. Bands like Jefferson Airplane, Big Brother and the Holding Company (featuring Janis Joplin) and the long-playing Grateful Dead created the "San Francisco Sound." The

taste for long hair, Indian religion, second-hand velvet, wind chimes, tambourines, incense and – if you knew where to go – free love.

Though the legacy of this wave of Utopian anarchy has been enormous, it

magazine *Rolling Stone* was founded, and a new visual language appeared on record sleeves and Pop Art posters. If you missed the party, Tom Wolfe's *The Electric Kool-Aid Acid Test* gives a lively account of those heady days.

Tea and sympathy: get your fortune told at Mad Magda's Russian Tea Rooms in Hayes Valley

historic ships – some are still undergoing loving restoration – and there are also demonstrations of boatbuilding skills and a well-stocked Maritime Store. The pier is the main attraction in the extensive San Francisco Maritime National Historical Park (see page 83), and provides fine views of the city, Alcatraz and Golden Gate Bridge.

C A Thayer
This three-masted schooner was built in 1895 to transport timber down the Pacific coast, then later used to carry salted cod and salmon. There is a telling contrast between the captain's cozy, wood-paneled dining room and the grim forecastle bunks, where up to 28 crew slept on six-month codfishing trips.

Eppleton Hall
This English-built paddle-wheel tug of 1914 is reminiscent of the vessels used in the Bay in Gold Rush times.

HAYES VALLEY
West of the Civic Center, the Hayes Valley is a resurgent neighborhood born out of freeways brought down by the 1989 earthquake. Since then it has developed a reputation as a showcase for young and innovative designers, with an easy-going strip of interior design shops, art galleries, cafés and restaurants.
Hayes Street by Laguna and Franklin Streets. Bus: 21.

HYDE STREET PIER
At the west end of Fisherman's Wharf, this is the best place to get a feel for San Francisco's maritime past. Moored up around the pier is a magnificent fleet of

Craftsman at work on Hyde Street Pier

Balclutha

Built in Scotland in 1886, this stately square-rigged sailing ship carried cargo round the Cape Horn 17 times and visited ports throughout the world. Its towering masts and creaking decks are a romantic advert for the ocean life – providing you resided in the extraordinarily plush quarters reserved for the captain and his wife.

Alma

This flat-bottomed scow schooner was built in 1891 and is typical of the vessels once used for transporting bulky products such as hay and bricks across the Bay.

> **BARBARY COAST**
>
> Prior to the 1906 earthquake, the area around Jackson Square became known as the "Barbary Coast," a reference to the lawless Mediterranean coast of North Africa where Berber pirates once roamed. It was here that the abundantly male population of the Gold Rush days spent their wages, letting off steam in streets thick with bars, brothels, gambling houses and opium dens. The verb "shanghai," where men were drugged and kidnapped to serve as hands on ships bound for the Far East, originates from this time.

Eureka

Hyde Street Pier originally served as a car ferry terminal, and this steam-powered paddle-wheel ferryboat provides a nostalgic passage back to life in San Francisco before the bridging of the Bay. Built in 1890, she carried railway cars and then automobiles, and operated a regular service between this pier and Sausalito.

A taste of life at sea on the SS *Balclutha*

North end of Hyde Street. Tel: 415/556–3002. Open: daily 10am–5:30pm (6pm summer). Admission charge. Cable car: Powell/Hyde. Bus: 32.

JACKSON SQUARE HISTORICAL DISTRICT

On the northern fringes of the Financial District, this protected area of predominantly 19th-century commercial buildings escaped the devastation caused by the 1906 earthquake. Its heart lies close to the Transamerica Pyramid, in Jackson Street between Montgomery and Sansome Streets, and is now occupied by antiques showrooms, law offices and small businesses. The 1866 Hotaling Building (451–455 Jackson Street) was originally a wholesale liquor firm.
Bus: 12, 15, 42.

JAPANTOWN

The origins of San Francisco's Japanese community date back to the start of this century, when migrants working in the Hawaiian sugar plantations moved on to the fields of California. Many of those that settled here found work in the shipping, retail and art trades, creating several pockets of Japanese life around the city. After the 1906 earthquake, a predominant number moved to the Western Addition, a neighborhood of Victorian housing west of Van Ness Avenue.

Following the Japanese attack on Pearl Harbor in 1941, many Japanese-Americans were forcibly deported from

The Peace Pagoda in the Japan Center is a focal point for the city's Japanese community

the city to internment camps in the desert. African-American migrants brought in to work in the shipyards moved into the Western Addition, and subsequent urban planning has left the heart of today's 12,000-strong Japanese community in a box of streets by the northeast corner of Geary Boulevard and Fillmore Street.

Japan Center

The focus of Japantown is the Japan Center, a five-acre shopping and entertainment complex opened in 1968. It has little of the hectic color of Chinatown's crowded alleys, but does offer an agreeable taste of Japanese culture in concentrated form. As it is mostly indoors, this is the sort of sight many tourists only get round to if it's raining.

The pivotal point is the 100-foot Peace Pagoda, a gift from the people of Japan and a backdrop for the Cherry Blossom Festival held here every April. As well as bookstores, art galleries, antiques shops and sushi bars, the Center includes the Kabuki Hot Spring, offering Japanese baths and shiatsu massage, the Kabuki 8 cinema (films are not in Japanese), and Elka's, an esteemed fish and seafood restaurant in the Miyako hotel.

Post and Buchanan Streets. Japan Center Information – tel: 415/922–6776. Open daily. Bus: 2, 3, 4, 22, 38, 38L.

JEWISH MUSEUM OF SAN FRANCISCO

The museum holds exhibitions on all aspects of historic and contemporary Jewish culture, and fosters links with Israel and Jewish communities throughout the world.

121 Steuart Street. Tel: 415/543–8880.

Neat street: the twists and turns of Lombard Street have become a popular tourist attraction

Open: Sunday 11am–6pm, Monday to Wednesday noon–6pm (8pm Thursday) Closed: Friday, Saturday. Admission charge. Metro: Embarcadero. Bus: 14, 32.

LOMBARD STREET

San Francisco's hills have given rise to "The World's Crookedest Street." Its eight curves snake down through flower beds in the space of a single block, and provide a favorite location for films, commercials and photo opportunities. The street is only open to descending traffic, with a staircase beside for pedestrians.

Lombard Street between Hyde and Leavenworth Streets. Cable car: Powell/Hyde.

MARITIME MUSEUM

An exquisite architectural gem, this sleek 1939 building standing on the south side of Aquatic Park forms part of the San Francisco Maritime National Historic Park (see page 83). It was designed by William M Mooser Jr to resemble a luxury liner and comes complete with streamlined decks, porthole windows and ship's wheel door handles. Inside are serene art deco murals of underwater life by Hilaire Hiler.

The building's original function was as the "Aquatic Park Casino," a bathing station for Aquatic Park. Today it houses a maritime museum with exhibits recalling San Francisco's seafaring past from the hearty era of whaling and Cape Horners to the prim days of steamships, yachting and commuting by ferryboat. Panoramic photos upstairs offer an engrossing comparison of the city in the 1850s and 1976.

North end of Polk Street at Beach Street. Tel: 415/556–3002. Open: daily 10am–5pm. Free. Cable car: Powell/Hyde. Bus: 19.

M H DE YOUNG MEMORIAL MUSEUM

We have Michael Harry de Young, editor of the *San Francisco Chronicle*, to thank for this fine art museum in Golden Gate Park. It was founded with profits from the 1894 California Midwinter International Exposition that he promoted in the park – a few sculptures from this chest-beating fair now stand outside. The collection opened in 1919, displaying works exhibited in the Exposition, and over the decades it has gathered together a substantial treasury of art from around the world.

Historic American art is the main attraction at the M H De Young Museum in Golden Gate Park

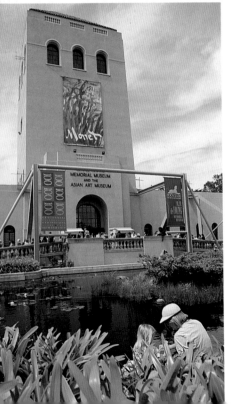

A floor plan and suggested chronological tour is available from the entrance hall. Exhibits change regularly, but the strength of the museum lies in its 22 galleries devoted to American art. These journey from the colonial period to contemporary works from the Bay Area, and have as much sociological interest as aesthetic. Portraits of the vain and influential are accompanied by examples of the furniture they perched on; landscapes reveal the romanticization of scenic spots like Mount Tamalpais ("the Pacific Parnassus"), the Golden Gate and a pre-computer age Santa Clara Valley.

Decorative arts from the Shaker and Arts and Crafts styles provide the most satisfying intimations of beauty. Other galleries, rather incongruously, offer treasures from the Classical world, a complete George III dining room, works by Gainsborough and Reynolds, and a miscellany of glass, textiles and art from Africa and the Americas.

The museum currently shares the same building as that housing the Asian Art Museum (see page 37). If plans for that museum to relocate in the Civic Center are achieved, the M H de Young is expected to expand into the vacated space.

Hagiwara Tea Garden Drive, Golden Gate Park. Tel: 415/863–3330. Open: Wednesday to Sunday 10am–5pm (8:45pm first Wednesday of month). Closed: Monday, Tuesday. Admission charge, but free first Wednesday and Saturday (10am–noon) of month. Bus: 5, 21, 44.

MISSION

Named after Mission Dolores (see page 72), San Francisco's Hispanic neighborhood offers visitors a complete and vivid immersion in the Spanish-speaking cultures of Mexico and Central

Eat, drink and go Hispanic in the Mission, the city's oldest and liveliest neighborhood

and South America. It was here and in the Presidio that the Spanish missionaries and colonists laid the foundations of modern San Francisco. After the Gold Rush the area was settled by German and Irish immigrants – the present Latino explosion started in the 1960s.

The Mission is bisected by the longest street in the city, Mission Street – the most enjoyably intense part lies between 16th and 24th Streets. In contrast to the orderly and introspective, drive-everywhere mentality that pervades so much of San Francisco, the fog-free streets here are a colorful parade ground thick with chat, fashion and play. Every shop, bar and *taqueria* proclaims its allegiance to the mother country – Argentine football shirts are on sale next to Guatemalan textiles, Cuban cocktails vie with Mexican *burritos*, even the pavements are decorated with saucy red and blue tiles.

Part of the excitement of the Mission comes from its colorful and dramatic murals, which invariably have a social or political message to expound. Balmy Street, south of 24th Street between Treat and Harrison Streets, is a typical example. This was the site of the neighborhood's first community mural, painted in 1973, and has vivid pictures on the theme of "Peace in Central America." There are now some 200 murals in the Mission – the best way to enjoy them is to take a guided tour (see page 30).
BART: 16th Street, 24th Street.
Bus: 12, 14, 14L, 26.

Mission Dolores: today a wedding cake basilica dwarfs the original adobe-walled mission

MISSION DOLORES

The Mission San Francisco de Asís is where the story of San Francisco begins. Dedicated to St Francis of Assisi, it was founded on June 29, 1776, by Father Francisco Palou, a student and colleague of Junípero Serra, the creator of the California Missions. He was traveling as part of a Spanish colonizing expedition of 34 families led by Juan Batista de Anza – the Presidio (see page 81) was established at the same time. The Mission's popular name results from a nearby lake known as Nuestra Señora de los Dolores (Our Lady of the Sorrows).

Mission Chapel

Constructed by Indians, the present Mission building was originally completed in 1791. Its adobe walls are four feet thick and made from an estimated 36,000 sun-dried bricks. The three bells are Mexican and date from the 1820s. The interior of the chapel is simple but colorful – the patterned design on the beamed ceiling is of Indian origin while the late 18th-century altar screen was brought from Mexico. Further artifacts from the Mission era are displayed in a small museum by the garden entrance, originally the Mission schoolroom.

Basilica

Rearing up beside the Mission Chapel like a monster kid brother who just discovered fashion, the Basilica was built between 1913 and 1918 to replace the previous church destroyed in the 1906 earthquake. It is decorated in neo-Churrigueresque style, imitating Spanish baroque at its most exuberant, and has windows depicting the 21 Californian Missions.

Cemetery

The harsh truth behind the romantic history of San Francisco is told by the tombstones in this graveyard. Many of its dead are Irish, buried at pitifully young ages in the late 19th century, and others from France, England and South America bear witness to the false hopes of immigration. Other plots belong to the victims of the vigilante gangs, self-elected lawmen who dealt out summary justice in 1850s San Francisco. In their midst a statue of Father Junípero Serra looks down at his weary feet, while another of the maiden Tekakwitha honors the thousands of nameless native American Indians buried in the area.

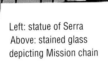

THE MISSION LINE

Mission Dolores was the sixth of 21 Missions founded by the Spanish in California. The first was founded in 1769 in San Diego and the last at Sonoma in 1823. Their founding Father was the Mallorca-born Junípero Serra, who was beatified by the Catholic Church in 1988. The Mission line was linked by El Camino Real (The Royal Road) – Highway 82 now follows it north from San Jose to San Francisco. The Missions, along with the Presidios built here and in Monterey and Santa Barbara, were used to convert the native Indians, and secure California for the Spanish Crown.

Left: statue of Serra
Above: stained glass depicting Mission chain

Many were killed by measles, a virus imported by the settlers.
16th and Dolores Streets. Tel: 415/621–8203. Open: daily 9am–4:30pm (4pm winter). Admission charge. Metro: J. Bus: 33.

MUSEUM OF MONEY OF THE AMERICAN WEST

The Bank of California was built in 1909 with all the sober, monumental classicism that a temple to money-making could muster in a post-earthquake city. Rows of Corinthian columns fence in its great banking hall, beneath which lies a small basement museum devoted to the money that won over the West. Displays include gold nuggets, historic banker's orders, commemorative medals, ingots, banking accessories and exhibits associated with the Comstock silver mines.
400 California Street. Tel: 415/765–0400. Open: Monday to Thursday 10am–4pm (5pm Friday). Closed: weekends. Free. Cable car: California Street. Bus: 1, 42.

Towers of power: Nob Hill has been an affluent neighborhood for over a century

to link with the Union Pacific Railroad at Utah, this pioneered a transcontinental transport link, completed in 1869, that secured their fortunes.

The 1906 earthquake erased their showy castles, but the legacy of these powerful men lives on. Three grand hotels now hoist their names into the skies – the Mark Hopkins Inter-Continental, the Stouffer-Stanford Court and the Huntington – while the Grace Cathedral (see page 62) stands on the site of Crocker's mansion. In their midst stands one haughty survivor, the dark chocolate Pacific-Union Club (1000 California Street). An exclusive gentlemen's club, it was built in 1886 for James Flood. He belonged to another wealthy quartet, the Irish "Bonanza Kings" who reaped the profits of the "Big Bonanza" vein of silver ore discovered in the Comstock mines in 1873. Memorabilia from the days of the Nob Hill's silver and railroad barons can be seen in The Big Four Restaurant at the Huntington Hotel (1075 California Street).

Cable car: Powell/Hyde, Powell/Mason, California Street. Bus: 1, 27.

NORTH BEACH

There's no beach at North Beach – that disappeared soon after the Gold Rush – just one of San Francisco's oldest and most likeable neighborhoods. Pizza parlors, aromatic cafés and tri-colored flags on the lamp-posts proclaim it as "Little Italy," but the feel and history of North Beach is much more variegated. It's been a Hispanic quarter, "Little Ireland," home to a Russian-Serbian Greek Orthodox church, a red-light district, jazz hotspot, the Beat

NOB HILL

One of the most prestigious addresses in America, Nob Hill's reputation as a luxury residential neighborhood owes much to the invention of the cable car. Prior to that the rich hogged the best level ground while the poor clambered up the hillsides. After the opening of the California Street line in 1878, this 338-foot peak overlooking the Financial District became both accessible and desirable.

By 1882, as Robert Louis Stevenson noted, it was a place where "millionaires are gathered together vying with each other in display." Its king was Leland Stanford, who along with Mark Hopkins, Charles Crocker and Collis P Huntington ("The Big Four") invested in the construction of the Central Pacific Railroad. Running east from Sacramento

Generation's training camp – now its one big eating and drinking party. The best way to crash it is by strolling northwest along Cristòforo Colombo (Columbus Avenue) to Washington Square – for a suggested walk see page 96.

North Beach Museum
On the mezzanine floor of the Eureka Savings Bank, this small museum documents the Irish, Chinese, Italian and Beat Generation influences on North Beach. Affectionate work by local residents, such as the photographs of John B Monaco and the hand-written poetry of Lawrence Ferlinghetti, help make this past feel human and accessible.
1435 Stockton Street at Columbus Avenue. Tel: 415/626–7070. Open: Monday to Thursday 9am–4pm, Friday 9am–5:30pm. Closed: weekends. Free.

Views across the Bay from the top of Nob Hill

Washington Square
The most watchable of the city's many small green spaces, Washington Square is pure San Francisco. Daily performances start with Chinese residents practising their early morning tai chi, followed by a cavalcade of gnarled old Italian men in suits, chirruping schoolchildren, book-devouring sunbathers and poetry-declaiming down-and-outs. Nightfall brings neon lights, packed restaurants and the illuminated beacon of Coit Tower.

The charm of the square owes much to the Church of Saint Peter and Saint Paul, dating from 1922, though tellingly, services here are now also conducted in Chinese. On the grass outside is a statue of Benjamin Franklin, and another by the children's playground pays tribute to the city's volunteer fire crews – paid for in 1933 by the fire engine-chaser Lillie Coit (see page 86).
Bus: 15, 30, 41, 45.

OCTAGON HOUSE

Offering plentiful daylight, the octagonally shaped house is a minor architectural fad that provoked some interest in Victorian San Francisco. This 1861 example houses a collection of colonial and federal-era furniture, antiques and ephemera.

2645 Gough Street at Union Street. Tel: 415/441–7512. Open: February to December on every second Sunday and Thursday and fourth Thursday of the month, noon–3pm. Closed: January. Donation requested. Bus: 41, 45.

OLD US MINT

Known as the "Granite Lady," this financial fortress in neoclassical disguise was constructed between 1869 and 1874 and proved sufficiently strong to survive

the 1906 earthquake. Silver and gold coinage were minted here until 1937.

Fifth and Mission Streets. Closed to public. Metro: Powell. Bus: 14, 14L, 26, 27.

PACIFIC HERITAGE MUSEUM

The museum celebrates the contribution of the nations of the Pacific Rim to the West with both changing and permanent exhibits. Its building forms part of the Bank of Canton of California and was originally the 1875 US Subtreasury, from which some original features survive. Displays are of a high quality and might cover subjects such as Thai costume, Chinese bronzes or the decorative traditions inspired by Buddhism. One room is given over to "Wings over the Pacific" featuring historic models of Boeing aircraft used on trans-Pacific routes.

Close by is the Chinese Historical Society at 650 Commercial Street (see page 95).

608 Commercial Street. Tel: 415/399–1124. Open: Monday to Friday 10am–4pm. Closed: weekends. Free. Bus: 1, 15.

PALACE OF FINE ARTS

Perhaps the eeriest of San Francisco's historic sights, this wilfully melancholy colonnade and rotunda are a legacy of the 1915 Panama-Pacific International Exposition. Ostensibly held to celebrate the opening of the Panama Canal linking the Pacific and Atlantic Oceans, the 10-month event also announced the return of the city to the world scene after the devastation of the 1906 earthquake.

While Europe descended into the blood and mud of World War I, San

The Palace of Fine Arts is a survivor of the buildings created for the Pan-Pacific Exposition

Francisco's Marina district became a party-box of national pavilions and funfair amusements. The centerpiece of the 635-acre site was a glittering Tower of Jewels, decorated with thousands of cut-glass colored beads and mirrors. Other exhibits included a working model of the Panama Canal and palatial halls devoted to worthy themes like Machinery, Horticulture and Education.

The Palace of Fine Arts was designed by Bernard Maybeck and stood at the west end of the Exposition. Built in Beaux-Arts style with classical columns, a reflective pool and cypresses, it was intended to evoke the dream-like grandeur of Roman ruins – the nymphs apparently checking the state of the roof reflect the sadness of "life without art." Though only built as a temporary structure, this much-loved monument survived until the 1960s, when a donation by a local resident enabled it to be permanently reinforced with concrete. The adjacent exhibition hall now houses the Exploratorium (see page 52.)

Marina Boulevard and Baker Street. Open access. Bus: 30.

It's all right for some: sea-lions basking in the sun (above) beside Pier 39 (below)

PIER 39

The big tourist magnet in Fisherman's Wharf (see page 53), this fun-for-all wooden-planked pier has two levels of cheek-by-jowl shops, restaurants and entertainments. With a carousel, simulated rides, street performers, toy shops and fast food outlets it is

particularly pleasing to children. Motorized cable car city tours and Bay cruises with the Blue & Gold Fleet also depart from here. The most baffling thing about Pier 39, which rather calls their taste into question, is the decision of many California sea-lions (billed as "sea-lebrities") to sunbathe on the decks of its West Marina.

Embarcadero at Powell Street. Tel: 415/981-7437. Shops open daily: 10:30am–8:30pm. Free. Cable car: Powell/Mason. Bus: 32.

PAINTED LADIES

In the second half of the 19th century San Francisco grew from a gold-diggers' tented city to a metropolis, as Rudyard Kipling found it in 1899, of "thousands and thousands of little houses made of wood, each house just big enough for a man and his family."

Abundant timber in the forests of the Bay Area provided the raw material for this new city, and advances in carpentry and construction methods enabled the mass production of a richly decorated terraced housing that is today collectively termed Victorian. Forty-eight thousand such houses were built between 1850 and 1915, and despite the fires following the 1906 earthquake and unsympathetic home improvements carried out in later decades, many "Painted Ladies" survive as matronly examples of this architectural heritage.

While stylistic diversity is a hallmark, Victorians fall into three predominant groups. Those built during the 1870s are often termed "Italianate" for their use of classical designs derived from the Italian Renaissance. They have flat roofs with detailed cornices, windows and door frames, and some have angular

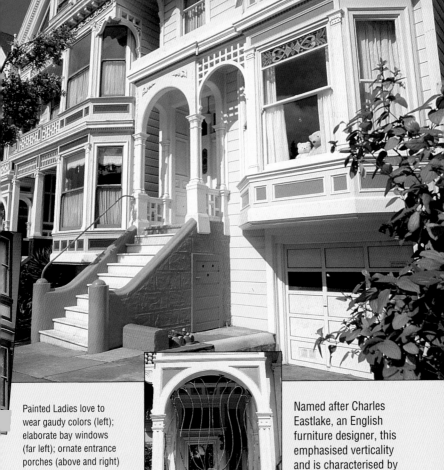

Painted Ladies love to wear gaudy colors (left); elaborate bay windows (far left); ornate entrance porches (above and right)

bay windows. The need for economical land use meant that many Victorians had to fit into a regular plot measuring 25 feet by 100 feet, and they often had similar floor plans. Elaborately painted and ornamented façades were therefore a main source of social distinction.

In the next decade the Stick (also known as Eastlake) style prevailed.

Named after Charles Eastlake, an English furniture designer, this emphasised verticality and is characterised by false gable roofs and square-sided bay windows. During the 1890s a third style, known as Queen Anne, was imported from the East Coast. These buildings also favoured gable roofs but incorporated elaborate asymmetrical designs such as a corner tower, rounded bay windows and decorative wooden shingles or patterned panels.

PORTSMOUTH SQUARE

With its early morning tai chi sessions, gaggles of chess and card-players and a children's playground bubbling with young life, Portsmouth Square has become the social focus of Chinatown (see page 46–7). An underground car park lies beneath its oppressive concrete, which can attract phenomenal lines on weekends when San Francisco's Chinese-American community returns to its roots to shop and dine. A memorial pays tribute to the Scottish author Robert Louis Stevenson, who lived in the city between 1879 and 1880, and liked to sit here and watch life go by.

Now lorded over by the Holiday Inn Hotel, it is hard to imagine what the square was like when it was the hub of Yerba Buena, the fledgling waterside settlement that preceded San Francisco. The community of "Good Herb" officially dates from 1835, when an English sailor, William Richardson, built a house on what is now Grant Avenue. American settlers came to join him, mixing with the Californios (California-born Mexicans) who had moved north in the wake of the Spanish colonists. On July 9, 1846, following the United States declaration of war against Mexico, the USS *Portsmouth* sailed into Yerba Buena Cove and hoisted the Stars and Stripes in this plaza. The Mexican forces in the Presidio surrendered peacefully, and six months later Yerba

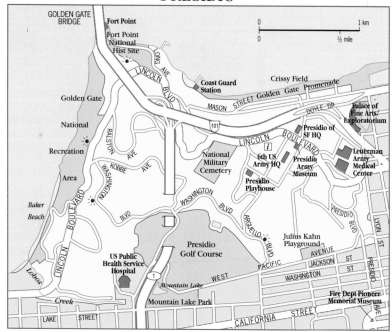

PRESIDIO

Chinese puzzle: chess and card players are a common sight in Portsmouth Square

Buena was renamed San Francisco. *Kearny and Washington Streets. Bus: 1, 15.*

PRESIDIO

The Presidio (fort) was founded by the Spanish in 1776 and until 1994 was the longest continuously operating military post in the US. In that year, as part of defence cuts ordered by Congress five years previously, its 1,480 verdant and historic acres were handed over to the National Park Service. Today the Presidio is part of the Golden Gate National Recreation Area, and being groomed to become "A Park for the 21st Century." The good intentions are that its military heritage will be preserved, its forests and shores opened up to public access, and its buildings given over to worthy cultural and educational institutions.

Information Center

With the park still evolving, the best way to enjoy the Presidio is to contact its Information Center in the Main Post. This is the heart of the military complex, with a historic parade ground where troops mustered for inspection for over two centuries. As well as providing guides and maps detailing the Presidio's buildings and nature trails, you can learn about the excellent weekend program of escorted walks, hikes and bike rides that unravel its military past.

The architecture of the Presidio is particularly interesting – some wooden buildings survive from the Civil War era, others are tricked out in 1910s Spanish Colonial style, and an original row of 1921 Pilots' Houses, built for the pioneering aviators of nearby Crissy Field, stands near the junction of Lincoln Boulevard and Long Avenue. There are also coastal defence batteries to explore and curiosities like the Pet Cemetery, created in 1945 for guard dogs but now a shrine to the family pet.

Presidio Visitor Information Center, Building 102, Montgomery Street. Tel: 415/561–4323. Open: daily 10am–5pm. Main gate at Lombard and Lyon streets. Bus: 28, 29, 43.

Memorial to Robert Louis Stevenson

·TO REMEMBER
ROBERT·LOVIS
·STEVENSON·

PRESIDIO ARMY MUSEUM

Built in 1862, the Presidio's former hospital is now a historical museum. Exhibits provide a revealing account of the Presidio in its formative Spanish days (1776–1821), as a troop embarkation center during the Spanish-American War (1898–1902), and as a refugee camp in the aftermath of the 1906 earthquake. Models depicting the mansions of Nob Hill and the pavilions built for the 1915 Panama-Pacific International Exposition are also on display. A shop has information and books about the Presidio and Golden Gate National Recreation Area (GGNRA), and at the rear are two wooden "cottages" built by the army and

Recruitment poster in the Presidio Army Museum

local carpenters for the post-1906 homeless. *Lincoln Boulevard and Funston Avenue. Tel: 415/561–4331. Open: Wednesday to Sunday 10am–4pm. Closed: Monday, Tuesday. Free. Bus: 29.*

RUSSIAN HILL

Working south from Alaska, Russian fur traders visited the coast of California at the same time as the Spanish were establishing their line of Missions. In 1812 a Russian hunting post was set up at Fort Ross, 60 miles north of San

Wooden-faced mansion in Russian Hill, a well-off, independent-minded neighborhood

Is it a bishop's hat or a half-buried bomb about to explode? No, it's St Mary's Cathedral

Francisco, and four years later a visiting artist, Ludovic Chloris, painted detailed scenes of native Indians dancing outside Mission Delores.

Russian Hill is thought to be so-named because it was where these Russian traders buried their dead. With superb views of the city and Bay, it is today as desirable a residence as Nob Hill next door, but has little of its ostentatious glitz. Here the atmosphere is one of affluent bohemia – one-off houses with roof terraces, steep wooded steps overgrown with ivy, a creative population. Literary San Franciscans such as Ambrose Bierce, Frank Norris, Ina Coolbrith (honored with a park) and Jack Kerouac have resided here, as well as the architect Willis Polk.

The southern summit of Russian Hill is by Russian Hill Place, at the junction of Jones and Vallejo Streets. Cable car: Powell/Hyde. Bus: 41, 45.

ST MARY'S CATHEDRAL

With its hilltop site, vast plaza and parabolic white walls sweeping up to 190 feet, St Mary's is a classic example of the way the architects of modern churches seek to provide spiritual uplift through daring structural engineering and innovative decorative symbolism. Built in 1971, it's interior can seat a 2,500-strong congregation and has the feel of a heaven-bound rocket ship. Abstract stained glass represents the four elements, but the eye is first caught by a space age baldachino suspended above the altar like silver rain, designed by Richard Lippold.

1111 Gough Street at Geary Street. Tel: 415/567–2020. Open: daily, but access restricted during services. Free. Bus: 38.

SAN FRANCISCO FIRE DEPARTMENT PIONEER MEMORIAL MUSEUM

Part of a working fire station in Pacific Heights, this enthusiastic collection of firefighting memorabilia includes several historic engines that wouldn't seem out of place in a silent movie. Early hydrants and extinguishers, helmets and uniforms, bugles and badges are accompanied by dramatic photographs of early conflagrations and volunteer crews.

655 Presidio Avenue at Pine Street. Tel: 415/861–8000. Open: Thursday to Sunday 1–4pm. Closed: Monday to Wednesday. Free. Bus: 2, 4, 43.

SAN FRANCISCO MARITIME NATIONAL HISTORICAL PARK

Offering insights into the maritime history of San Francisco, the park is spread over several locations including Hyde Street Pier, the Maritime Museum, SS *Jeremiah O'Brien* (Fort Mason Center) and USS *Pampanito* (see individual entries).

Reflect on modern art at the new SFMOMA, part of the redevelopment around Yerba Buena Gardens

SAN FRANCISCO MUSEUM OF MODERN ART

In 1995 SFMOMA moved from the Civic Center to new purpose-built galleries in Yerba Buena Gardens designed by the Swiss architect Mario Botta. The museum is now only second to New York's MOMA in the space it can devote to exhibiting modern art, and has already proved its determination to be at the cutting edge of cultural debate. You might be shocked by what you see, but you won't be disappointed.

Galleries are on four levels and combine travelling shows with a rotating selection from SFMOMA's considerable collection of quality modern art and sculpture. Smart picture-gazers will take the elevator to the top and work down. Space is also given to photography, architecture, film and special projects, and there is a well-stocked Museum Store and Caffè Museo.

SFMOMA Collection

In the 60 years prior to this triumphant relocation, SFMOMA has acquired works by many of the leading artists of our century, some of which will always be on view. European masters represented include Picasso, Cézanne and Matisse, whose 1905 *Femme au Chapeau* is probably the most renowned painting in the museum. Paul Klee, American Abstract Expressionists like Jackson Pollock and Clyfford Still, and the work of contemporary Bay Area artists are other fine art strengths.

The photography collection includes work by leading Americans such as Alfred Stieglitz, Imogen Cunningham and Ansel Adams and the European Surrealists. In a city of stunning architecture, it is natural that the likes of Bernard Maybeck (designer of the Palace of Fine Arts), Willis Polk, Frank Lloyd Wright and Timothy Pfleuger are

represented, while an entire room created by the furniture designers Charles and Ray Eames is one of the museum's most unique acquisitions.
151 Third Street (between Mission and Howard streets). Tel: 415/357–4000. Open: Tuesday to Sunday 11am–6pm (9pm Thursday). Closed: Monday. Admission charge, but free first Tuesday of the month. Metro: Montgomery. Bus: 9, 12, 14, 15, 30, 45, 76.

SAN FRANCISCO ZOOLOGICAL GARDENS

At the southern end of Ocean Beach, the grounds of San Francisco Zoo cover a 125-acre site. Opened in 1929, it works hard to be a modern-thinking city zoo providing optimum conditions for both visitors and residents. The range of species of birds and mammals is vast, but the monkey business in the Primate Discovery Center and the quasi-human citizens of Gorilla World are particular favorites. Koala Crossing and Penguin Island are other popular spots, while Big Cat Feeding (2pm daily except Monday) allows close inspection of lunching lions and tigers.

A Children's Zoo offers hands-on interaction with farm animals and nature trails, and a Zebra Train provides half-hour tours of the entire menagerie.
Sloat Boulevard at 45th Avenue. Tel: 415/753–7083. Open: daily 10am–5pm. Children's Zoo 11am–4pm. Admission charge, but free first Wednesday of month. Metro: L. Bus: 18, 23. For suggested bus ride see page 102.

Animal magic awaits at San Francisco Zoo

MURAL ART

Murals have become a feature of San Francisco's artistic heritage. The colourful frescos of the Mexican painter Diego Rivera (1886–1957) bedeck walls in the former Pacific Coast Stock Exchange, San Francisco Art Institute and City College, where a vast Panamerican Mural commissioned for the 1939 Golden Gate International Exposition depicts leading figures from the 1930s. The influence of his bold, social realist style can be seen in the Depression-era murals in Coit Tower, and in the vivid political comment of contemporary street murals in the Mission district. Tours are arranged by City Guides (see page 30).

Above: Telegraph Hill is crowned by the Coit Tower and a statue of Columbus (right)

TELEGRAPH HILL

With commanding views over the Bay, this hill was the site of a semaphore erected in 1850 to signal the arrival of ships. Quarrying into the sides explains its cliff-like aspects. Today the summit is accessible by road or a steep walk. See North Beach walk, pages 96–7.

Coit Tower

Telegraph Hill would probably be just another park but for Lillie Hitchcock Coit (1843–1929), who had a deep fascination with fires and firefighters – the superheroes of her day. In girlhood she became the mascot of the Knickerbocker Hose Company No 5, and as an adult frequently dressed up in uniform to attend the city's blazes. On her death she left a healthy sum intended for "adding to the beauty of the city," which resulted in Coit Tower.

Inevitably likened to the nozzle of a fire-hose, this 210-foot tower was completed in 1933. A lift takes visitors to enjoy the views from the top, but the interior murals are equally eye-catching. Commissioned as a Public Works of Art Project to provide employment during the Depression, they depict life in California with a rich documentary detail, particularly Victor Arnatoff's masterly *City Life*. Their political comment was deemed so strong that the tower was closed during the violent dockers' strike of 1934.

Tel: 415/362–0808. Open: daily 10am–6:30pm. Admission charge. Bus: 39. Parking is very limited with long lines at popular times. To walk up see page 97.

TELEPHONE PIONEER COMMUNICATIONS MUSEUM

Built in 1925, the headquarters of the Pacific Telephone and Telegraph Company epitomizes the strange, Utopian beauty that the best art deco skyscrapers exude. An island of historic charm just south of Market Street, it was co-designed by Timothy Pfleuger, architect of fantasy movie palaces in the Castro and Oakland and the stunning office block at 450 Sutter Street.

The black marble entrance lobby has a lively oriental dream ceiling, while to the right lies this eccentric museum devoted to the evolution of telephone communications. As well as the expected antique telephones and switchboards, there are informative displays on the Chinatown Telephone Exchange and an extraordinary phone-in pioneered at the 1915 Panama-Pacific International Exposition that enabled partygoers wearing copper-soled shoes and headsets to call home as they danced.

140 New Montgomery Street, Suite 111. Tel: 415/542–0182. Open: Monday to Friday 10am–2pm. Closed: weekends. Free. Metro: Montgomery. Bus: 9, 14, 71.

TRANSAMERICA PYRAMID

This 48-story, 853-foot pyramidal tower is the city's tallest building. When it was completed in 1972 by William Pereira and Associates, it was likened to a "corporate teepee" and "a spike driven through from Hell": now it is a much-loved city landmark.

The building serves as an emblematic headquarters for the finance and insurance company Transamerica Corporation. Like many modern beat-the-next-earthquake towers, its floors and foundations are designed to move with the tremors rather than resist them. Art acquisitions are displayed in the foyer, while outside the Transamerica Redwood Park provides a half-acre urban refuge and venue for lunchtime concerts.

600 Montgomery Street. Tel: 415/983–4000. Open: Monday to Friday 8:30am–4:30pm. Closed: weekends. Admission free. Concerts usually run May to September on Fridays at noon, call to confirm. Bus: 1, 15, 41, 42.

Once ridiculed, the Transamerica Pyramid is now one of the most loved buildings in the city

TREASURE ISLAND

Two miles east of the city, the island of Yerba Buena provides a stepping stone for the 8.5-mile San Francisco–Oakland Bay Bridge. It has been the property of the US Navy since 1898 and is now partly used by the US Coastguard. To its north is a flat, 400-acre artificial island built in 1939 to stage the Golden Gate International Exposition, which celebrated the opening of the Bay and Golden Gate Bridges. The new island was partly constructed with stone removed from the road tunnel on Yerba Buena Island, and was scheduled to become San Francisco's airport. With the escalation of World War II it was converted into a naval base. Now surplus to defence requirements, Treasure Island will probably be returned to the city in 1997.

Treasure Island Museum

During the brief time that Treasure Island functioned as an airport, the 1938 Admiralty Building served as the terminal for Pan Am's trans-Pacific China Clipper service – you can still see the old control tower on top. Today the building is a museum with exhibits about that romantic flying boat link, the 1939 Exposition, and the work of the US Navy, Marines Corps and Coastguard Service. Though the displays are rather disparate, many individual items bring the past alive – such as a lens shipped from Paris to the Farallon Islands lighthouse in 1854, an 1890 Gatling Gun, photographs of the Bay Bridge under construction and underwater atomic bomb tests in the Marshall Islands.

Naval Station Treasure Island, 410 Palm Avenue. Tel: 415/395–5067. Open: daily 10am–3:30pm. Admission charge. Bus: AC Transit.

View to Yerba Buena Island, site of the Treasure Island naval station and Bay Bridge

The eye-catching Sutro Tower on Mount Sutro, by Twin Peaks, carries television antennae

seat in Washington Square or Aquatic Park. It functions instead like a floral decoration in the center of a dining table – a pretty, inoffensive ornament to gather around.

Union Square gets its name from being a rallying point for supporters of the Union in the run-up to the Civil War (1861–5). Today its lawns mask one of the world's earliest multi-level underground car parks, designed in 1924 by Timothy Pfleuger. At its center stands a 90-foot column commemorating Admiral Dewey's triumph over the Spanish Navy in the Philippines in 1898, topped by a bronze depicting *Victory.*
Powell and Geary Streets. Cable car: Powell/Mason, Powell/Hyde. Metro: Powell. Bus: 2, 3, 4, 30, 45, 76.

TWIN PEAKS

When it's not foggy, the 360-degree views from this double-summit 913-foot hill are stupendous, with San Francisco spread out below like a child's board game. Dream street plans for the city were laid down from a house near this vantage point by the architect Daniel Burnham. After working for two years, he presented his grand project to the city authorities in 1905, only to have it scuppered by the great earthquake.
To drive here see 49-Mile Scenic Drive, page 106. Bus: 36, 37.

UNION SQUARE

Boxed in by top name department stores and the historic Westin St Francis Hotel, Union Square is the hollow heart of San Francisco's Downtown. Despite its formal gardens, benches and clanging cable cars, the square has little of the easy city charm that makes visitors take a

In the center of Downtown, Union Square is a park where shoppers can rest their feet

UNION STREET

Once known as Cow Hollow, the stretch of Union Street between Van Ness and Steiner Streets is now a prettified shopping strip fusing the moneyed neighborhoods of Marina and Pacific Heights. Its spruced up Victorians are a rainbow of chic boutiques, bountiful food shops, bijou gift stores, Italian and American restaurants and up-market hang-outs for affluent singles. If you like to stroll around small-scale shops with like-minded people, pausing for a drink here and a little purchase there, this is the place.
Bus: 41, 45.

USS *PAMPANITO*

Part of the San Francisco Maritime National Historical Park (see page 83), this US Navy submarine was built in 1943 and made six Pacific patrols during World War II. Clambering around its engine rooms, torpedo bays and confined living quarters gives a frightening insight into life on board. All submarine crews were volunteers, and the contribution to the war made by those who fought beneath the waves aboard "SS383" is recalled in an informative self-guided audio tour.

The USS *Pampanito* sunk six Japanese ships, including one discovered to have been carrying British and Australian prisoners-of-war. The submarine rescued 73 survivors from the engagement. Today the vessel is open to the public as a tribute to the thousands of missing submariners "still on patrol."
Pier 45, Fisherman's Wharf. Tel: 415/929–0202. Open: daily 9am–6pm (9pm summer). Admission charge. Bus: 32.

WELLS FARGO HISTORY MUSEUM

Wells, Fargo & Co. was founded in 1852 to provide banking and transport services between California and the eastern United States. As this museum emphatically proves, the story of the

The only way is up: once an urban wasteland, Yerba Buena Gardens is now a thriving arts complex

Gold Rush and the company's famous stagecoaches are indeed the stuff of Wild West movies. Gold nuggets, scales, miners' lamps and early banknotes bring home the realities of the prospectors' world, while the growth of the "Golden State" is recorded in exhibits on subjects like the Bear Flag Revolt, the growth of the telegraph system, and the exploits of robbers such as Black Bart, who always liked to leave a poem behind after a hold-up.

420 Montgomery Street at California Street. Tel: 415/396–2619. Open: Monday to Friday 9am–5pm. Closed: weekends. Free. Cable car: California Street. Bus: 15.

YERBA BUENA GARDENS

The building of Yerba Buena Gardens and its arts centers has been a crucial factor in the rebirth of the SoMa district (meaning South of Market Street).

Stagecoach in the Wells Fargo Museum – proof that the Wild West existed before John Wayne

Spread over and around the 1981 Moscone Convention Center, it already includes the Center for the Arts, San Francisco Museum of Modern Art, the Ansel Adams Center for Photography and the Cartoon Art Museum (see individual entries). Future plans will add a Mexican Museum, a base for the California Historical Society, and a Children's Center with an ice rink and bowling lanes.

The center of the complex is laid out with gardens and walkways mined with modern sculpture. On the south side the Martin Luther King Jr Memorial pays tribute to the assassinated civil rights campaigner with a 50-foot wide waterfall and panels engraved with his words. On the level above, the Sister Cities Garden incorporates plants from San Francisco's 13 sister cities, which range from the Irish city of Cork and Abidjan, capital of the Ivory Coast, to Sydney, Australia.

Mission Street at 3rd and 4th Streets. Metro: Powell. Bus: 9, 14, 15, 30, 45, 76.

Downtown

This walk plunges into the heart of San Francisco, an intense grid of streets crammed with department stores, office and hotel complexes and the sublime skyscrapers of the Financial District. Time the walk for a weekday, when the Financial District is in full swing. *Allow 1 hour.*

The walk starts in Hallidie Plaza, at the junction of Powell and Market streets. From the urban stage of the cable car turnaround, walk north up Powell Street to Union Square.

1 UNION SQUARE
Bounded by the Westin St Francis hotel and leading department stores, the square is named from the pro-Union rallies held here in the days of the Civil War (see page 89).
Leave the square at its southeast corner, crossing the road to walk north up Stockton Street. Turn right into Maiden Lane.

2 MAIDEN LANE
With its designer shops, art galleries and tables and chairs set out for lunching executives, Maiden Lane bears little resemblance to the notorious street of brothels that flourished here until the 1906 earthquake. The Circle Gallery at No 140 was designed in 1948 by Frank Lloyd Wright.
Cross Grant Avenue and continue to Kearny Street. Turn left, then right down Post Street to enter the Crocker Galleria.

3 FINANCIAL DISTRICT
Now you are amidst the neck-cricking world of San Francisco's business community. The 1982 glass-vaulted Crocker Galleria

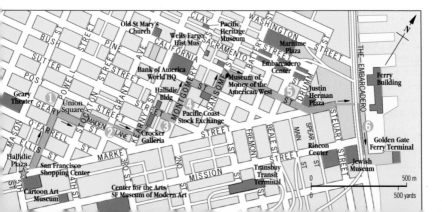

Walk between some of San Francisco's tallest buildings in the city's Financial District

takes its cue from the Galleria Vittorio Emanuele in Milan. At its northern end, at 130 Sutter Street, stands the Hallidie Building designed by Willis Polk in 1917. Framed with ornate metal cornices, its façade is a pioneering example of the glass curtain wall. *Turn right down Sutter Street to reach Montgomery Street, then turn left.*

4 MONTGOMERY STREET

The shore of Yerba Buena Cove ran close to this street before new land was claimed from the sea after the Gold Rush. The city's first banking street boasts several historic skyscrapers, such as the 1892 Mills Building at No 220 and the 1928 Russ Building opposite at No 235. Turn right down Pine Street to pass the grey Pacific Coast Stock Exchange at No 301, designed by Miller and Pfleuger in 1930.
Turn left at Sansome Street and walk along to California Street.

5 CALIFORNIA STREET

On the corner is the neoclassical Bank of California, designed in 1908 and now incorporating the Museum of Money of the American West (see page 73). Turn right to walk the length of California Street. With its cable car line climbing up to Nob Hill, the street has always been a prestigious address. The Tadich Grill at No 240 retains the atmosphere of old San Francisco. As you near Market Street you will see the Embarcadero Center to the left and ahead the Hyatt Regency Hotel.
At the junction with Market Street turn left towards the Ferry Building.

6 EMBARCADERO

To the left you will pass Justin Herman Plaza, with its squashed spider fountain designed by Armand Vaillancourt in 1971. In the park to the right is a statue of King Carlos III of Spain. Cross to the Ferry Building (see page 51) and follow the signs to the right for the Golden Gate Ferry. These end by a quay with superb views of the Bay Bridge.
There are bus stops and a Metro/BART station at the end of Market Street.

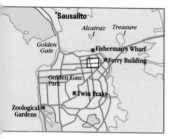

Chinatown

San Francisco's best-known neighborhood is safe, compact and packed with life and color. This introductory walk around its main sights reveals the history in its hectic streets. See also pages 46–7. The ideal time is on a Tuesday to Saturday afternoon, when the Chinese Historical Society is open. *Allow 90 minutes.*

The walk starts at the southern entrance to Chinatown at the junction of Grant Avenue and Bush Street.

1 CHINATOWN GATE

The Chinatown Gate, roofed with green tiles and animated dragons, welcomes visitors to the neighborhood's principal street, Grant Avenue. Built in 1970, the gate is part of a continuing effort to enhance the commercial image and tourist appeal of Chinatown.

Walk up Grant Avenue to the corner of Pine Street. Turn right and cross the street into St Mary's Square, next to Quincy Street.

Walking through you pass a steel-cloaked statue of the revolutionary Nationalist leader Dr Sun Yat-Sen, who lived in Chinatown prior to the overthrow of the Manchu dynasty in 1911.

2 OLD ST MARY'S CHURCH

On the corner of Grant Avenue and California Street rises the redbrick Roman Catholic church of Old St Mary's. Dedicated in 1854, its first congregations were predominantly Irish. A solemn warning on the clocktower – "Son, Observe the Time and Fly from Evil" – still advises visitors to flee the brothels and opium dens that once made Chinatown notorious. Lunchtime concerts are held here on Tuesdays at 12:30pm.

Turn right into Grant Avenue. At the next junction turn left up Sacramento Street, then right into Waverly Place.

3 WAVERLY PLACE

One of the most delightful streets in Chinatown, Waverly Place begins with the First Chinese Baptist church. Its dark, rubble-faced walls were constructed with bricks salvaged from the debris of the 1906 earthquake. Many of the buildings here were built by Chinese benevolent associations and incorporate temples in their upper floors. *Cross Clay Street. At the end of Waverly Place turn left into Washington Street, then immediately right into Ross Alley.*

4 ROSS ALLEY

Typical of the narrow alleys hidden within Chinatown, Ross Alley is a reminder of the backstreet sweatshops where many Chinese women work. A sweet biscuity smell wafts from the Golden Gate Fortune Cookie Company at No 56 – despite their traditional association with Chinese cuisine, the cookie with an inner motto was actually invented in 1909 by the Japanese manager of the Tea Garden in Golden Gate Park.
Turn right down Jackson Street to reach Grant Avenue. Turn right and walk one block, turning left into Washington Street. Note the ornate Bank of Canton at No 743, formerly the Chinatown Telephone Exchange (see page 46). Continue into Portsmouth Square.

5 PORTSMOUTH SQUARE

This historic square is now the social focus of Chinatown, see page 80.
Cross the square to reach Kearny Street. Turn right, cross Clay Street, then turn left down Commercial Street.

6 CHINESE HISTORICAL SOCIETY

Next to the Grabhorn Park gardens, at 650 Commercial Street, this small but highly informative museum documents the Chinese community's contribution to the story of San Francisco (see page 46). You might also visit the Pacific Heritage Museum at 608 Commercial Street (see page 76).
Walk back up Commercial Street to reach Grant Avenue. Turn left to return to the Chinatown Gate.

Built before the rise of Chinatown, Old St Mary's was San Francisco's first cathedral

North Beach

Proudly Italian, North Beach is best known for its restaurants, coffee bars and neon nightlife. Daylight reveals a much more dappled community, gradually succumbing to the benign advances of Chinatown and increasingly nostalgic for the Beat Generation it nurtured in the 1950s. This walk rolls down Columbus Avenue, then climbs Telegraph Hill for classic views over the city. See also pages 74–5. *Allow 90 minutes excluding time spent in bars and cafés, which could add a couple of days.*

The walk starts by the Transamerica Pyramid on the junction of Montgomery Street and Columbus Avenue.

1 COLUMBUS AVENUE

From the Transamerica Pyramid (see page 87), walk northwest up Columbus Avenue to pass the Sanwa Bank, a 1909 flatiron building that was the earlier home of the Transamerica Corporation. Cross Jackson Street, Kearny Street and Pacific Avenue, passing the fringes of Chinatown. Look out on the left for the Vesuvio Café and City Lights Booksellers at Nos 255 and 261, both hang-outs for Beat poets in the 1950s and now divided by Jack Kerouac Street.

The junction with Broadway, overseen by a vast mural

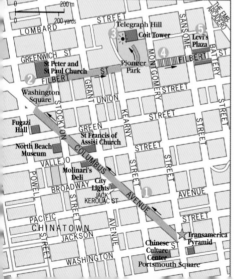

romanticizing North Beach life, marks the sleazy corner of the neighborhood. After crossing Grant Avenue and Vallejo Street, you meet the St Francis of Assisi church, followed by a gregarious parade of Italian restaurants, delicatessens and cafés, where it would be rude not to stop for at least a coffee. If you ever get to Green Street, take a last look back to the skyscrapers of Downtown, then follow Columbus Avenue as it rolls gently down towards the sea.
Cross Union Street into Washington Square.

2 WASHINGTON SQUARE

One of the best places to sit and watch San Francisco go by, the square is lit up

The leafy wooden steps
of Filbert Street

by the St Peter and St
Paul Church, designed
in 1922 and still a focal
point for San
Francisco's Italian-
American community.
*Cross to the northeast
corner of Washington
Square to climb up Filbert
Street. A stiff but short
climb culminates in steps
to the top of Telegraph
Hill.*

3 TELEGRAPH HILL

Follow the road
upwards for Coit
Tower and its splendid
murals and panoramic
views (see pages 86–7).
*Return to the original
route and continue left
down Filbert Street
Steps.*

4 FILBERT STREET STEPS

Superb views out to Treasure Island and
the Bay Bridge accompany the descent to
the sea. The very individual houses and
cottages lining these steps exemplify how
pockets of country living survive in the
midst of the city. As you cross
Montgomery Street, No 1360 is a
splendid 1936 art deco house with
etched glass, silver reliefs and a painted
figure of Humphrey Bogart in the
window that recalls its use as a location
in the 1947 crime film *Dark Passage.*
*Continue down the wooden steps, then cross
Sansome Street into Levi's Plaza.*

5 LEVI'S PLAZA

Designed in 1982, the plaza houses the
headquarters of Levi Strauss & Co,
purveyors of the world-famous denim
jeans first manufactured in the Gold
Rush. If you are here during office hours,
have a look at the period examples
displayed on the foyer's History Wall. At
the opposite corner of the plaza, the
Italian restaurant and bakery Il Fornaio
is a good place to recover from your
mountaineering.
*Bus 42 runs south from Battery Street to
Downtown, or north to Fisherman's Wharf
from Sansome Street.*

Sausalito
Alcatraz Treasure
I
Golden
Gate   Fisherman's Wharf
Ferry Building
Golden Gate
Park
Twin Peaks
Zoological
Gardens

Golden Gate Park

Founded in 1870, Golden Gate Park is a country
in the midst of a city. This walk introduces its
most popular features. See also pages 60–1. *Allow
from 90 minutes to half a day depending on how
many museums and gardens you visit. Leave the
park well before dark.*

*The walk starts at the northeast corner of Golden Gate Park at
the junction of Fulton and Stanyan Streets. Take Bus 21 from
Market Street.*

1 TO THE CONSERVATORY OF FLOWERS

A path leads from the corner of Fulton and Stanyan Streets
into the park, curling down through the woods to Conservatory
Drive. Cross this and continue straight on down the hill to a
crossoads of four paths by a green bench. Turn right and keep
on the path, which emerges by the dahlia beds on the east side
of the Conservatory of Flowers (see page 60).

2 TO THE M H DE YOUNG MEMORIAL MUSEUM

From the main entrance of the Conservatory of Flowers, walk
down the steps and bear right along a path to John F Kennedy
Drive. Cross this road and turn right to walk along the adjacent
path, marveling at the relentless parade of joggers, skaters,
roller-bladers, mountain bikers and even the odd walker. On
the left you pass the John McLaren Rhododendron Dell with a
statue of the devoted Scots park superintendent who shaped its
landscape. This is followed by the upstanding figure of
Chaplain William D McKinnon, then the Scots poet Robert
Burns, and, turning left into Hagiwara Tea Garden Drive, the

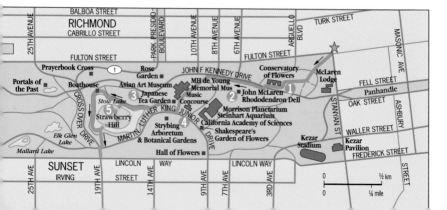

Reverend Thomas Starr-King. Continue past the statues of Junípero Serra and Miguel de Cervantes.

3 TO THE JAPANESE TEA GARDEN

The M H de Young Memorial Museum (see page 70) and Asian Art Museum (see page 37) stand to the right. Opposite is the California Academy of Sciences (see page 39). Continue along Hagiwara Tea Garden Drive, passing a pair of sphinxes and *The Cider Garden Press* – all statues surviving from the 1894 California Midwinter Fair. The shell-shaped bandstand, officially known as the Spreckels Temple of Music, dates from 1899. Beyond the museums is the Japanese Tea Garden (see page 60).

4 TO THE STRYBING ARBORETUM

From the Japanese Tea Garden walk down to Martin Luther King Jr Drive and turn right. Opposite is the Strybing Arboretum (see page 61).

5 AROUND STOW LAKE

When you leave the Arboretum, cross the road again and take the path straight ahead. This runs round beside the Japanese Tea Gardens. Turn left by their exit to walk up a hill and some steps. Turn right at the top, following a curving path that brings you to Stow Lake. Cross the road and bear right to walk beside the water. In the center of the lake is the 428-foot artificial island

Strawberry Hill, and a Chinese pagoda – a gift from the city of Taipei.

The walk continues around the lake, past the boathouse where boats can be hired. A more energetic route is to cross the Roman bridge to climb Strawberry Hill for its views of the city, emerging by the rustic bridge on the south side. From this point walk downhill, past some rest rooms, to the jarringly busy junction of 19th Avenue and Lincoln Way.

Bus 71 from the opposite side of Lincoln Way goes back to Market Street.

Stow Lake encircles the artificial island of Strawberry Hill and has boats for rent

Fisherman's Wharf

Cable cars have been carrying locals and visitors around the city since 1873, and are a quintessential feature of San Francisco. This tour (see map on pages 32–3) rides the famous lines linking Downtown and Fisherman's Wharf. Early in the morning or at sunset are the most magical times for this ride. *Allow 90 minutes excluding time spent in line.*

The ride starts in Hallidie Plaza, at the junction of Powell and Market Streets.

1 HALLIDIE PLAZA

Named after the inventor of San Francisco's cable car system (see page 26), the focus of the plaza is a manually operated turnaround for the cars. In high season long lines are inevitable, for no visitors leave San Francisco content unless they have ridden a cable car. This tour starts with the more popular Powell/Hyde line (marked "Beach & Hyde" on the front), but you will not miss anything if you follow the itinerary in reverse and take a Powell/Mason car (marked "Bay & Taylor" on the front).

2 POWELL/HYDE LINE

Try to sit or stand by the open-air seats on the right-hand side. The car travels north past Union Square, then climbs Nob Hill to halt by the Fairmont Hotel and the crossover with the California Street line. The descent down Powell Street offers views north across the Bay to Angel Island and east to the towers of the Financial District.

After swinging left along Jackson

Cable cars descending Powell Street

Street, the car turns into Hyde Street. The undulating streets ahead seem perfect for a classic San Francisco car chase. To the left are the woods of the Presidio, to the right Lombard Street, part of which is the famous "Crookedest Street" (see page 69). From here it is an exhilarating descent to the sea – ahead you can see the tall ships of Hyde Street Pier, with Alcatraz beyond.

Disembark at the final stop and walk down Hyde Street towards the sea.

3 FISHERMAN'S WHARF

Fisherman's Wharf is packed with restaurants, shops and attractions and can seem oppressively commercial when very busy. One antidote is to pause for a spell in Aquatic Park (see page 37) to the left, or inspect the evocative historic ships of Hyde Street Pier (see page 66) ahead. Turn right into Jefferson Street for the main parade. On the right you pass two shopping complexes, The Cannery (see page 41) and, by Leavenworth Street, the Anchorage Shopping Center. Continue past the bubbling seafood stalls, souvenir shops and fishing boats to reach the center of Fisherman's Wharf – heralded by a sign resembling a ship's wheel.

Turn right into Taylor Street. Three blocks south, at the junction with Bay Street, is the Powell/Mason cable car terminus.

4 POWELL/MASON LINE

Try to sit on the left of the car. The return ride begins with a swing left down

Yes, it's here – start spending now

Columbus Avenue, offering glimpses of Washington Square, Coit Tower and the Transamerica Pyramid. The car then turns into Mason Street, climbing up Russian Hill towards the Mark Hopkins Hotel. Passing the Cable Car Barn and Museum from which the entire system is controlled (see page 38), the ride swings into Powell Street and travels along the western side of Chinatown. After climbing up to the California Street junction, the car rolls back towards Market Street, providing fine views across the south of the city center.

The ride concludes at Hallidie Plaza.

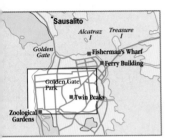

Ocean Beach

Buses provide a simple and inexpensive way of touring San Francisco. This three-bus circuit travels from Downtown to Ocean Beach to explore the untouristy western half of the city. This route (see map on pages 20–1) is based on weekday timetables only – you may want to buy a MUNI Passport before setting off (see page 23). *Allow 2½ hours, excluding time in the zoo.*

The bus ride starts at the southwest corner of Union Square, at the junction of Geary and Powell Streets. The 38L bus stop is in Geary Street, opposite Lefty O'Doul's restaurant.

Ocean Beach

1 UNION SQUARE TO POINT LOBOS

Board a 38L bus with "Point Lobos" on the front – and no other! At weekends the 38 bus travels the same route. Running the entire length of Geary Boulevard, "The Geary" cuts through San Francisco's mixed communities. After the bright lights of Union Square and the Theater District come the rough edges of the Tenderloin and, crossing Van Ness Avenue, a climb up to St Mary's Cathedral and Japantown.

Further west lie the multicultural residential rows of Laurel Heights and the Richmond district – Clement Street, a block further north, is rapidly growing into a second Chinatown. Look out on the right for the gold onion domes of the Russian Orthodox Holy Virgin Cathedral, on the corner of Geary Boulevard and 26th Avenue. The Russian community here dates from an influx of 10,000 immigrants after the 1917 Revolution.

Alight at the junction of Point Lobos and 48th Avenues.

The Castro – one of San Francisco's more colorful neighborhoods

2 OCEAN BEACH

Walk downhill towards the sea. On the left you pass Sutro Heights Park. This and the ruins of Sutro Baths and Cliff House ahead are the legacy of the property tycoon Adolf Sutro (see page 50). If it's cold and windy, Louis's Café, on the right at 902 Point Lobos Avenue, is the best place on the ride for a drink or snack. Continue downhill to enjoy the austere sands and exhilarating breezes of Ocean Beach.

Turn left into Balboa Street, then right into La Playa Street. The 18 bus stop is by Cabrillo Street, opposite Safeways.

3 OCEAN BEACH TO SAN FRANCISCO ZOO

Board an 18 bus. This travels south past the windmills of Golden Gate Park – first the complete Dutch Windmill built in 1902, then the sail-less Murphy Windmill of 1905. Both were used to pump water for the park up to a reservoir on Strawberry Hill. The bus then continues down 46th Avenue through the low-rise, pastel-toned suburbia of the Sunset district. This residential area developed in the 1930s, providing family homes with garages for the new automobile age. Relentlessly middle class, it is known as the "Fog Belt" because of the summer fog – that engulfs it.

Alight by the entrance to San Francisco Zoo in Sloat Boulevard.

4 RETURN FROM L

For San Francisco Zoo see page 85. To reach the L Metro stop, taking you back to Downtown, walk north up 46th Avenue to the junction with Wawona Street. The streetcar runs eastward on the surface along Taraval Street as far as West Portal Station, then burrows underground. If you want to explore another neighborhood, take a stroll around the Castro (see page 42) two stops further on.

The L Metro line continues to Embarcadero. Alight at Powell Street station for Union Square.

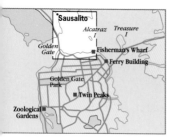

Sausalito

San Francisco's exceptional combination of cityscape, countryside and seashore makes cycling here a pleasure. This leisurely ride runs west from Fisherman's Wharf to cross Golden Gate Bridge and return by ferry from Sausalito. For Red & White Fleet ferry times call 415/546–2628. *Allow 3 hours.*

The ride starts by Hyde Street Pier, at the junction of Hyde and Jefferson Streets.

1 AQUATIC PARK TO MARINA GREEN

Follow the seafront path from Hyde Street Pier west around Aquatic Park. The curl of its Municipal Pier provides fine views

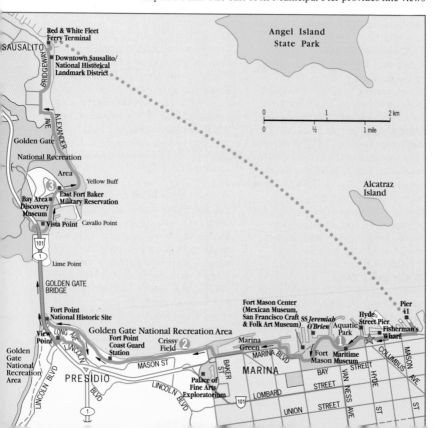

of Alcatraz. Turn left up a hill, marked "Bay Trai,", toward Fort Mason. From its top you can look down on the Liberty ship SS *Jeremiah O'Brien* (see page 57). Continue into the park, following the red paths past the statue of Congressman Phillip Burton, the environmental campaigner credited with the creation of the Golden Gate National Recreation Area in 1972. Ride downhill past the entrance to the Fort Mason Center, then continue west to the quays of the Marina Small Craft Harbor and the sports-crazed stage that is Marina Green.

2 CRISSY FIELD TO THE GOLDEN GATE BRIDGE

Turn right by Baker Street, passing Il Kiosko to reach the sea. Bear left and follow the water's edge to Crissy Field, which served as a military airfield between 1921 and 1936. After passing through some gates by the Old Coast Guard Station, you reach Fort Point National Historic Site, always popular with local fishermen. Continue along the chain-lined Marine Drive to Fort Point (see page 58).

Return towards Fort Point Wharf and take Long Avenue uphill to Lincoln Boulevard. Turn right, then follow the signs to Golden Gate Bridge. A path leads through the woods to the View Point and entrance to the bridge (see page 59). *Cyclists are directed to cross by different sides of the bridge at varying times during the week. If you take the west side, turn left at the far end of the bridge to cycle beneath it and join the coastal road*

(Conzelman Road) running east to East Fort Baker. If you cross on the east side, take the exit (Alexander Avenue) immediately after the Vista Point and follow the brown-and-white signs to the Bay Area Discovery Museum.

3 EAST FORT BAKER TO SAUSALITO

East Fort Baker was part of a complex arsenal of gun batteries and coastal fortifications built in the first half of this century to protect the Golden Gate, with barracks and quarters nearby for the soldiers who staffed them. For the Bay Area Discovery Museum, see page 153.

From the parade ground and coastguard station, Fort Baker Road leads north to Sausalito (also marked "Bay Trail"). Join the main road (Alexander Avenue) into Sausalito, marked with green "Bike Route" signs. This weaves through the town to reach the National Historical Landmark District. Turn right down El Portal to reach the Red & White Fleet ferry terminal. For Sausalito see page 116. *There is no charge for bicycles on the ferry, which in busy times board first and leave last. The Red & White Fleet ferry docks at Pier 41 on Fisherman's Wharf. To return to Hyde Street turn right and cycle along Jefferson Street.*

CYCLE HIRE

Bikes can be rented nearby from American Rentals, 2715 Hyde Street. Tel: 415/931–0234. A deposit is required.

49-Mile Scenic Drive

The 49-Mile Scenic Drive was created for visitors to the 1939 Golden Gate Exposition. Now updated and marked with blue-and-white seagull signs, it offers a thorough and enjoyable introduction to San Francisco's 47 square miles. Sunday is the best day; otherwise avoid the rush hour traffic. *The drive could be completed in 4 hours, but it is better to devote the best part of the day.*

The circuit can be picked up at any point and followed counter-clockwise. This itinerary starts by the Ferry Building at the junction of Embarcadero and Market Street.

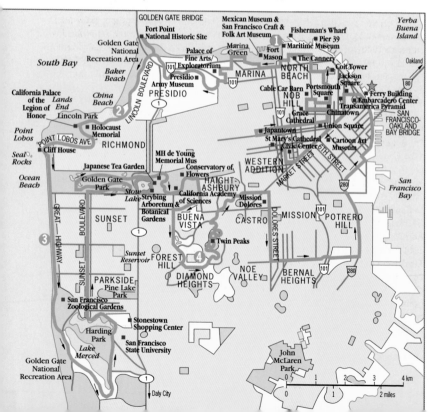

1 DOWNTOWN TO FISHERMAN'S WHARF

Drive north and turn left into Washington Street, then Battery Street. Continue down to Market Street and turn right. At the Civic Center take Hayes Street to join Van Ness Avenue. Get in the left lane for Geary Boulevard and follow the seagulls to loop around Japantown, returning east along Post Street. This leads down to the Financial District and a left turn up Grant Avenue through the gateway to Chinatown. Turn left up the steep incline of California Street to Nob Hill. The drive continues via Taylor, Washington, Clay and Kearny Streets to Columbus line and North Beach. Turn right up Grant Avenue for Telegraph Hill and Coit Tower. Unless there is a long line of traffic, this is a good spot to stop for air and superb city views (see page 86). Pick up the route again in Lombard Street and continue to Fisherman's Wharf.

2 AQUATIC PARK TO CLIFF HOUSE

Follow the coast west via Jefferson, Beach and Bay Streets. After passing Fort Mason and Marina Green (look out for the turning left up Scott Street), the drive winds past the Palace of Fine Arts and into the Presidio. Continue along Lincoln Boulevard to view Fort Point and Golden Gate Bridge. Return to Lincoln Boulevard, following the cliffs to pass the golf course in Lincoln Park and take Point Lobos Avenue to Cliff House.

Road signs indicate the route of the 49-Mile Scenic Drive

3 OCEAN BEACH TO GOLDEN GATE PARK

Continue downhill to drive the length of Ocean Beach, passing San Francisco Zoo to follow John Muir Drive around Lake Merced. Turn left into Lake Merced Boulevard, driving north past Harding Park to take Sunset Boulevard to Golden Gate Park (see page 60). Road signs direct you on a comprehensive tour through the park to emerge at its east end at Stanyan Street.

On Sundays John F Kennedy Drive from 19th Avenue to Stanyan Street is closed to traffic. Follow the signs for the alternative route along Martin Luther King Jr Drive to exit Golden Gate Park at Stanyan Street.

4 HAIGHT-ASHBURY TO TWIN PEAKS

Now follow the seagulls' winding ascent of Twin Peaks via 7th Avenue and Laguna Honda Boulevard. From the summit, unless it is foggy, you can see the city spread out below. The descent cuts between Haight-Ashbury and the Castro via Roosevelt Way and 14th Street to savor the palm-lined splendor of Dolores Street. If you arrive before 4pm, you could visit Mission Dolores (see page 72).

Compared to what you have just enjoyed, the rest of the drive hardly merits its "Scenic" title. If you like the bitter end, continue along Army Street, turning left on to Highway 280 to curl back to the Embarcadero.

BRIDGING THE BAY

The Golden Gate Bridge and the San Francisco–Oakland Bay Bridge (commonly known as the Bay Bridge) were both opened within six months of each other – a sensational double act born of visionary engineering, the rise of the automobile, and a surge of civic pride that culminated in the Golden Gate International Exposition on Treasure Island in 1939.

Work began on both bridges in 1933, with the 8.5-mile Bay Bridge opening first in November 1936. It is in fact two bridges: a suspension bridge spanning the waters between the Embarcadero and Yerba Buena Island, and a cantilever section bounding over to the Oakland waterfront. It carries 250,000 cars a day.

The 1.7-mile Golden Gate Bridge opened in May 1937, and has become a world-famous city emblem that is still a thrill to cross. Its chief architect was Joseph Strauss, who built over 400 bridges. His several assistants are credited with its elegant art deco design, which makes light of the monumental construction tasks the bridge required. Sinking the piers on which its two 746-foot towers rest was a feat similar to building skyscrapers underwater. Essential trivia: in high winds the roadway can sway up to 27 feet in the center; the bridge is forever being painted in a color known as International Orange; it takes four years to apply a complete coat; most suicides face the city.

Another three main bridges cross the waters of the Bay. The oldest is the southern Dumbarton Bridge, first built in 1927 but replaced with the present steel skeleton in 1984. In the north is the 5.5-mile Richmond–San Rafael Bridge. Connoisseurs of bridge experiences should also seek out the San Mateo Bridge, opened in 1967, which links San Mateo and Hayward. Spanning 6.8 miles, its eastern section comprises a level slipway that gives a divine feeling that you are driving on water.

Cathedrals for cars: the Bay Bridge (above) and the Golden Gate Bridge (right)

Around the Bay

The big thrill of the Bay Area is its scenic variety. Even though parts of it are laced with freeways and dormitory conurbations, there are abundant opportunities to lose yourself in nature and have fun. Imperious redwood forests, bountiful wine valleys, wild mountains and soothing country parks, the sandy beaches and breezy headlands of the Pacific coast – all these can be visited comfortably in a day trip from San Francisco.

If you have the time to take things easy, spend a night in the Sonoma Valley or by Highway 1. If time is short, a trip to Muir Woods is instantly refreshing.

Such accessible natural beauty makes a car both essential and desirable, but remember that you can easily take the BART to Berkeley and the ferry to Oakland. If you're heading off to beaches, woods and parks for the day it's best to have a picnic on board and a full petrol tank. In the summer potential fire hazards can lead to the closure of back roads and parks, so call ahead for the latest situation.

Head North for the Marin Headlands

BAY AREA

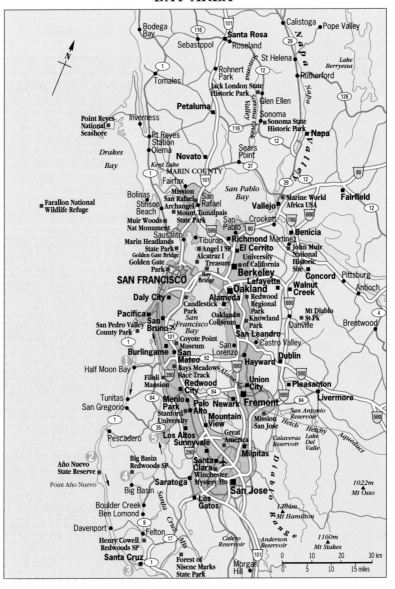

North Bay

BERKELEY

Draped on the ridges of the East Bay,
Berkeley has always lived in thrall to
"Cal" the University of California
created in 1868 and one of the most
famous in America. Its reputation owes
much to the wealth and energy of its
benefactress Phoebe Hearst, wife of the
mining tycoon George Hearst and
mother of press baron William
Randolph, who pumped in over $15
million worth of support. Today it has
around 21,000 students, a tally of seven
Nobel Prizewinners, and a graduation
rate of 77 percent – the highest on
record.

Campus Tours

The 1,232-acre campus is a brain-
soothing parkland with serene lawns and
graceful academic buildings. The
hushed progress of students between
lecture halls and seminar rooms makes it
hard to believe that the same university
was a hotbed of protest in the 1960s and
early 1970s, vehemently supporting the
civil rights movement and nationwide
demonstrations against the Vietnam
War.

A map and guided or DIY tours are
available from the Visitor Center at the
corner of Oxford Street and University
Avenue. A useful early target is the 307-
foot Sather Tower, modeled on the
bell-tower of St Mark's Square in
Venice, which offers sweeping views in
all directions from an observation
platform. Other key sights worth seeking
out are the aesthetic 1907 Hearst
Mining Building, the Bancroft Library,
which has a small museum of
Californian history, and Berkeley's

traditional meeting and ranting venue,
Sproul Plaza.

*Visitor Information Center, 101 University
Hall, 2200 University Avenue. Tel:
510/642–5215. Tours leave on Monday,
Wednesday and Friday at 10am and 1pm.
Sather Tower open in term-time Monday to
Saturday 10am–3:15pm, Sunday
10am–1:30pm. Admission charge. Closed:
call for opening times during University
holidays.*

Lawrence Hall of Science

Mainly catering to schoolchildren, this
interactive museum hides in the hills
above the main campus, linked by a
shuttle bus from Hearst Mining Circle.
Exhibits are on science-is-fun themes like
insects, the human brain and DNA as a
molecular playground.

*Centennial Drive. Tel: 510/642–5132.
Open: daily 10am–4:30pm (5pm
weekends). Admission charge.*

Phoebe Hearst Museum of
Anthropology

This small but quality museum displays
changing exhibits from its far-ranging
collection of anthropological and
archaeological treasures. One part tells
the story of Ishi, "the last Californian
Indian," who came in from the
mountains in 1911 to live in the museum
(then based in San Francisco) and pass
on invaluable knowledge about the crafts
and lore of his Yahi tribe. He died five
years later from tuberculosis.

*103 Kroeber Hall, Bancroft Way at College
Avenue. Tel: 510/643–7648. Open:
Wednesday to Sunday 10am–4:30pm (9pm
Thursday). Closed: Monday, Tuesday.
Admission charge but free on Thursdays.*

Above: the campus at Berkeley; right: food for thought on Telegraph Avenue

Telegraph Avenue
The spirit of the Sixties lives on in the hippy craft stalls lining Telegraph Avenue – just. The four blocks that matter run south from Sproul Plaza to Dwight Way. Once a nexus of militant protest and riot, they are now a sad and histrionic strip where street traders selling tie-dye shirts and labor-intensive jewelry mix with drunks, punks and students doing disappointingly normal things like buying books, stationery and computer gadgetry.

University Art Museum
Stimulating and provocative exhibitions are guaranteed in this spacious, fan-shaped art gallery, which also has a permanent collection of work by the abstract colorist Hans Hofmann.
2626 Bancroft Way at College Avenue. Tel: 510/642–0808. Open: Wednesday to Sunday 11am–5pm (9pm Thursday).

Closed: Monday, Tuesday. Admission charge but free Thursday 11am–noon, 5–9pm.

12 miles east across Bay Bridge. BART: Berkeley. Bus: AC Transit. Berkeley Convention & Visitors Bureau, 1834 University Avenue. Tel: 510/549–7040.

Literary den in the House of Happy Walls, now a museum celebrating the life and work of Jack London

JACK LONDON
STATE HISTORIC PARK

Born in San Francisco, raised in Oakland, Jack London (1876–1916) lived for adventure and writing. At one time the highest paid author in the US, his novels, journalism and short stories dealt in the fundamental human dramas he witnessed during an itinerant life that included prospecting in the Klondike Gold Rush and sailing a ketch to the South Pacific.

In 1911 he and his wife Charmian moved to a 1,400-acre estate near Glen Ellen which he christened "Beauty Ranch." Here he continued writing and supervising the construction of Wolf House, a dream home that mysteriously burnt down close to completion. Three years later he died, but his wife continued to stay in a new home, the House of Happy Walls, until 1955.

Today this is a faithful museum to London, while part of the ranch is now a tranquil park that includes farm buildings and the writing "cottage" where he died. *47 miles north at Glen Ellen, for directions see page 124. Tel: 707/938–5216. Museum open: daily 10am–5pm, park from 8am. Admission charge.*

MARIN HEADLANDS
STATE PARK

A curtain of green hanging on the northwest side of Golden Gate Bridge, the Marin Headlands are a remarkably wild and unspoilt sanctuary for wildlife and de-stressing city victims. The best touring route is clockwise, stopping first at Battery Spencer for a stupendous view back to San Francisco. Continue west along the one-way Conzelman Road. The remains of gun emplacements along the coast are a legacy of the long military presence here, which also protected the headlands from attack by developers. Today they are part of the Golden Gate National Recreation Area.

The road winds on west to a stop overlooking Point Bonita Lighthouse, built in 1874. Continue north to the Visitor Center at the east end of Rodeo Lagoon, which occupies the former military chapel. Information is available on the trails, horse-riding, bird-watching and beaches to be enjoyed in the area. To return to civilization drive east along Bunker Road.

Marine Mammal Center

On the north side of Rodeo Lagoon a former missile site is now a hospital-cum-orphanage for seals and sea-lions. It is run by volunteers, and visitors are welcome to observe the mammals' treatment and recuperation.
Tel: 415/289–7325. Open: daily 10am–4pm. Free.

Take the Alexander Avenue exit on the north side of Golden Gate Bridge. Visitor Center, tel: 415/331–1540. Open: daily 9:30am–4:30pm. Bus: 76 on Sunday only.

MARINE WORLD AFRICA USA

Wildlife shows, an oceanarium and a family fun theme park come together in 160 acres of animal-packed action. Attractions include Bengal tigers, elephants, chimpanzees, alligators, a walk-in aviary and butterfly habitat, a Dinosaur Adventure and a rare opportunity to travel through a transparent acrylic tunnel while sharks, rays and tropical fish whizz overhead.
30 miles northeast via Interstate 80 and

Highway 37. Ferry: Red & White from Pier 41 or Ferry Building. Tel: 707/643–6722. Open: daily in summer 9:30am–6:30pm (5pm winter). Closed: Monday and Tuesday in winter. Admission charge.

MOUNT TAMALPAIS STATE PARK

See page 136.

MUIR WOODS NATIONAL MONUMENT

Muir Woods National Monument provides many visitors with their first experience of the majesty of redwood trees. Named after John Muir (1838–1914), the champion of forest conservation in the United States, this 491-acre arboreal heaven lies at the foot of Mount Tamalpais and is a rare example of first-growth coastal redwood forest. An easy trail leads from the Visitor Center around some of its mightiest denizens.
12 miles north via US 101 and Highway 1. Visitor Center, tel: 415/388–2596. Open: daily from 8am to sunset. Free.

Whales are just one of the many natural stars performing at Marine World Africa USA

Wildflowers in the Napa Valley

NAPA VALLEY

America's premier wine region has become a parade of showcase vineyards where you can spend many merry hours tasting quality wine, picnicking on lawns, ballooning, comparing winery architecture, learning about viticultural processes and admiring fine art and sculpture. Quite a few visitors even come here to buy some wine.

The greatest density of wineries stretch north along Highway 29 between Napa and Calistoga. Locals will tell you that it's best to only visit a few of them and to avoid the weekends when there are crowds and traffic jams, but no one listens. For a suggested tour see page 125.
47 miles northeast via US 101.

POINT REYES NATIONAL SEASHORE
See pages 136–7.

SAUSALITO

Welcome to "The Geneva of America," as a 1910 tourist brochure once boldly described this relaxed and affluent waterfront town. Sausalito's proximity to the Golden Gate Bridge and the Marin Headlands, backed by regular ferry connections to San Francisco, makes it a soft target for tourists taking a trip on the Bay. The views back to the city are marvellous, and there are plenty of bars and restaurants where you can enjoy a leisurely meal looking out at the boats on the Bay. It can get very crowded at weekends.

Bay Area Discovery Museum
See page 153.

San Francisco Bay and Delta Model
To the north of town, this enormous computer-controlled scale model of San Francisco Bay, constructed by the Army Corps of Engineers for scientific research, diligently reproduces every ebb and flow of its tidal waters.
2100 Bridgeway. Tel: 415/332–3870. Open: Tuesday to Friday 9am–4pm, weekends 10am–6pm. Closed: Monday, Sunday in winter. Free.

8 miles north. Take Alexander Avenue exit from US 101 north of Golden Gate Bridge. Ferry: Red & White from Pier 43½, Golden Gate from Ferry Building. Bus: Golden Gate Transit.

SONOMA VALLEY

If the Napa Valley is a young and ever-smiling hostess in a designer business suit, then the parallel Sonoma Valley likes the laid-back, smart-jeaned, mature and natural look. Its wines are just as fine, the atmosphere in the vineyards less intense, but the big difference is that Sonoma has history – and it knows it.

The town of Sonoma was founded in 1823, marking the northern end of the Mission line the Spanish started building from San Diego in 1769. Its spacious central plaza also witnessed the never-to-be-forgotten Bear Flag Revolt of 1846, which proclaimed the independent republic of California that lasted for almost a whole whopping month.

Sonoma State Historic Park
The key buildings in the town's history are now part of the Sonoma State Historic Park. In the northeast corner of the central Plaza stands the restored Mission San Francisco Solano de Sonoma. Just across 1st East Street stands its two-story barracks, which now house a museum and Visitor Center. The Victorian home of General Vallejo, the Mexican commander overthrown by the Bear Flag revolutionaries, is a short drive west along Spain Street.
Tel: 707/938–1519. Open: daily 10am–5pm. Admission charge.

45 miles north, see page 124. Bus: Golden Gate Transit. Sonoma Valley Visitors Bureau, 453 1st Street East. Tel: 707/996–1090.

TIBURON
Like Sausalito, Tiburon is a lazy, riviera-style pleasure port that oozes well-being. Ferry connections with San Francisco and nearby Angel Island (see page 136) make it a popular objective for an easygoing cruise or cycling tour. There's not much to do, save browse the shops along Main Street and Ark Row and drink in the Bay views from waterfront deck cafés.
12 miles north via US 101 and Highway 131. Ferry: Red & White from Pier 43½ or Ferry Building. Bus: Golden Gate Transit.

The good life: pleasure boats in Tiburon

South Bay

FILOLI MANSION

This stately home was designed by Willis Polk in 1915 for the wealthy San Franciscan gold mining magnate William Bowers Bourn II. The property reflects its owner's admiration for the country estates of Ireland, and is named from the first letters in his favorite motto: "Fight for a just cause, Love your fellow man, Live a good life." The 43-room house includes a ballroom decorated with scenes from Killarney, while the surrounding 654-acre estate includes splendid mature gardens, a tea room and gift shop.

25 miles south via Interstate 280, take Canada Road exit. Tel: 415/364–2880. Open: Tuesday to Saturday from mid-February to early November. Closed: Sunday, Monday. Guided tours only – book first. Admission charge.

MOUNT DIABLO STATE PARK

Extraordinary views over the Bay Area are the worthwhile reward for negotiating the bottleneck freeways and urban sprawl that gnaw the flanks of this 3,849-foot mountain on the western edge of Central Valley. The summit is accessible by car (watch out for kamikaze chipmunks) but also gained with astonishing ease by local mountain-bikers. Around this lies the gentle wilderness of the park, with panoramic picnic spots, trails and campsites. The Park Office is at the junction of North Gate Road and Mount Diablo Scenic Boulevard.

Information is also available from the small museum inside the summit watchtower. *33 miles east via Walnut Creek. Take Diablo Road exit off Interstate 680 at Danville. Tel: 415/837–2525. Open: 8am to dusk. Views can be hazy in summer. Admission charge for vehicles.*

Country house splendor at Filoli Mansion

OAKLAND

If you've fallen madly in love with San Francisco, Oakland is like taking the cold but necessary shower. The city is easily reached via the Bay Bridge, but the best introduction is to arrive by ferry, which passes the mammoth docks and naval yards of one of the largest ports on the West Coast. As drugs and crime are a problem in this depressed area, it is best to stick to busy and well-lit streets.

Jack London Waterfront

The ferry from San Francisco berths by Oakland's equivalent to Fisherman's Wharf, named in homage to the writer Jack London (see page 114). Bear right to reach Jack London Square. Beyond it is the log cabin where he lived while prospecting in the 1897 Klondike Gold Rush. Further on, in the timber shopping center of Jack London Village, a small museum recalls his life and work.
Ferry: Blue & Gold from Ferry Building or Pier 39. Tel: 415/705–5444.

Downtown

From Jack London Square, Broadway runs north under the Nimitz freeway to the architectural miscellany of the city center. On the right, between 8th and 9th Streets, is Oakland's Chinatown, free of the gaudy, tourist-pleasing trappings adopted in San Francisco. Shimmering skyscrapers point to new investment in the heart of the city, but its most poignant buildings are those left from the dream-filled days of the 1930s, notably the Paramount Theater at 2025 Broadway designed in 1931 by Timothy Pfleuger. Another eye-catching landmark is the 1923 Tribune Tower on 13th and Franklin Streets, former home of the *Oakland Tribune* newspaper.
BART: 12th Street. Bus: AC Transit.

Dream-time at the Paramount Theater, Oakland

Oakland Museum of California

A walk east along 11th Street brings you to this functional three-level museum where you could easily spend several hours enjoying a comprehensive account of the ecology, history and art of California. The history galleries are the most engrossing, cruising smoothly from native Indian culture and the gold-crazed 1850s into the modern world of Beats, hippies and computer whizz-kids. A bookstore, cafeteria and rooftop sculpture gardens lighten the burden of self-education.
Oak and 10th Streets. Tel: 510/238–3401. Open: Wednesday to Saturday 10am–5pm, Sunday 12pm–7pm. Admission charge. BART: Lake Merritt.

On the east side of the Bay Bridge. Oakland Convention & Visitors Bureau, 550 10th Street, Oakland, Suite 214. Tel: 1–800/262–5526.

Groves of academia: the serene campus
of Stanford University, Palo Alto

Quad is a cathedral-like shrine to the
family. For an overview of the campus
take the lift up the 285-foot Hoover
Tower, a short walk to the east. A small
museum at its base pays homage to
Stanford's most famous student, the
Republican President Herbert Hoover.
The 1989 Loma Prieta earthquake
damaged several buildings in the
University, including the Stanford
Museum of Art on Lomita Drive which
remains closed. Some consolation is
provided by the Rodin Sculpture Garden
outside, which is richly populated with
the French artist's work.
*33 miles southeast on US 101. Rail:
CalTrain. Bus: SamTrans. Take University
Avenue south past the railway station.
Stanford University, tel: 415/723–2300.
Main Quad Information Center open in
term-time daily 10am–4pm. One hour
guided tours on weekdays at 11am and
3:15pm. Hoover Tower Observation
Platform open daily 10am–11:45am and
1–4:30pm. Closed: call for opening times
during University holidays.*

PALO ALTO

Stanford University
Founded in 1885 by the railway baron
Leland Stanford, this is one of America's
top private universities with some 13,000
students and close links to the adjacent
Silicon Valley. The main entrance to the
8,180-acre campus is via Palm Drive on
its north side. This leads to its charming
centerpiece, the neo-Romanesque
arcaded Main Quad. There is a Visitor
Center here where you can pick up a
map.
  The University opened in 1891 and is
dedicated to Stanford's son Leland Jr,
who died of typhoid aged 15. The
Memorial Church on the far side of the

PARAMOUNT'S GREAT AMERICA
Scenes from the films made by
Paramount Pictures provide the theme
for this thrill-giving 100-acre family
entertainment park. Attractions include
adventure rides inspired by *Top Gun* and
Days of Thunder and children's shows
starring Yogi Bear, the Flintstones and
the *Star Trek* crew.
*45 miles southeast on US 101, take Great
America Parkway exit. 3 miles north of San
Jose. Tel: 408/988–1776. Open: daily in
summer and irregular dates rest of the year.
Park opens 10am, closing times vary.
Admission charge.*

POINT AÑO NUEVO
Año Nuevo State Reserve

This coastal wildlife reserve is best known for its elephant seals, but whalewatching and seabirds are other draws. The main breeding season for the 7,000 seals that gather in orgiastic heaps on Bight Beach, and in the abandoned lighthouse buildings of Año Nuevo island just offshore, is between December and March. At this time access is only by guided walk with reservations necessary, but you can also see seals here at other times. All visitors must get a permit from the Visitor Center.

Highway 1, see page 126. Tel: 415/879–0227. Open: daily April to September 8am–6pm, October and November 8am–4pm, December to March for guided walks 8:15am–3:15pm. Charge for vehicle and walks.

SAN MATEO

Coyote Point Museum for Environmental Education

Just south of San Francisco airport, this is an excellent waterside museum explaining the natural history of the Bay Area. Core exhibits illustrate the seven major habitats in the region with the help of resident wildlife stars ranging from indolent rattlesnakes and banana slugs to hyper-athletic river otters. Few museums provide such a meaningful explanation of the natural world as this – while jumbo jets tear through the skies above.

1651 Coyote Point Drive. Tel: 415/342–7755. Open: Tuesday to Saturday 10am–5pm, Sunday noon–5pm. Closed: Monday. Admission charge.

17 miles south on US 101. Rail: CalTrain. Bus: SamTrans.

Bobcat (below) and badger (right) at the Coyote Point Museum for Environmental Education

SAN JOSE

San Jose may lack the compact, great city feel of San Francisco, but the capital of Silicon Valley does have several unique sights worth catching if you're in the mood.

Rosicrucian Museum

The American headquarters of the Rosicrucian Order, whose members draw inspiration from a mystical and esoteric philosophy that flourished in ancient Egypt, can be found in serene, campus-like grounds to the west of Downtown. Papyrus groves and statues of animal deities stand outside an Egyptian Museum modeled on the temples at Karnak. Exhibits include many artifacts from the days of the Pharaohs, including a walk-in replica of a step pyramid, and a Planetarium.

1342 Naglee Avenue. Tel: 408/947–3635. Open: daily 9am–5pm. Admission charge.

Tech Museum of Innovation

Motivated by a desire to explain in layman's terms the wonderful but often baffling inventions that have emerged from Silicon Valley, this museum puts great faith in enlightenment through interaction. Visitors are invited to step into a machine to count their dust particles, watch the manufacture of a silicon chip, have a portrait drawn by a robot, make a DNA fingerprint and design a dream mountain bike. A CD-ROM Infolounge provides a gulp-making opportunity to experience the virtually real life to come.

145 West San Carlos Street. Tel: 408/279–7150. Open: Tuesday to Sunday 10am–5pm. Closed: Monday. Admission charge.

Winchester Mystery House

In 1884, following a meeting with a Boston pyschic, the tormented and reclusive daughter-in-law of the inventor of the Winchester rifle set builders to work on a never-ending madhouse that would hopefully appease the spirits of people killed and injured by the company's firearms. Carpenters worked round the clock for the next 38 years until her death, creating a 160-room Addams Family-style luxury residence using the very best materials.

The result is spooky mayhem.

The spirit of ancient Egypt lives on in the Rosicrucian Museum in San Jose

Figuring it out in the Tech Museum in San Jose

Skylights in the floor and chimney breasts that stop short of the roof, flights of steps two-inches high, staircases that rise into the ceiling, doors leading to thin air. Sounds like a gimmick? Well 10,000 windows, 2,000 doors, 52 skylights, 47 fireplaces, 40 staircases, six kitchens, three elevators, two bathrooms and a shower would argue different.
525 South Winchester Boulevard. Tel: 408/247–2000. Open: guided tours daily 9:30am–4pm. Admission charge.

50 miles southeast on US 101. Rail: CalTrain. Bus: Greyhound. San Jose Convention & Visitors Bureau, 333 West San Carlos Street, Suite 1000. Tel: 408/295–9600.

SANTA CRUZ
Santa Cruz has been a classic American seaside resort since the creation of its funfair Boardwalk in 1907. With its safe, sandy beach, historic amusements and a pier jutting into Monterey Bay, the town is a good place to pause while driving Highway 1 – and a must if you have children on board.

Santa Cruz Beach Boardwalk
A jubilant 1911 Looff Carousel and a screaming 1924 Giant Dipper rollercoaster are the star attractions in this well-organized parade of seaside thrills. Discover the culinary mysteries of beef jerky, salt water taffy, gyros and funnel cakes as you tread the boards to a Beach Boys soundtrack. The Historium on the second floor of Neptune's Kingdom gives a fascinating historical account of the Boardwalk and the good old days when crowds flocked to see Mighty Bosco perform a "Stratosphere Dive" from 80 feet up into water only eight-feet deep.
400 Beach Street. Tel: 408/423–5590. Open: Memorial Day to Labor Day, most weekends and holidays. Admission charge for rides.

74 miles south on Highway 1, see page 126.

Having some fun on the Boardwalk, Santa Cruz – a traditional seaside resort

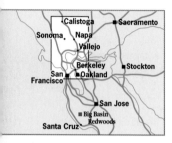

Wine Valleys

For many visitors to San Francisco a trip to the Napa Valley, the amiable headquarters of the American wine industry, is as essential as a cable car ride. This 150-mile round tour, which also visits the less commercial Sonoma Valley, offers a very Californian blend of wine-tasting, culture and picnics on the lawn. *Allow a full day, starting early.*

This itinerary begins, as all great journeys should, on the Golden Gate Bridge.

1 MARIN COUNTY

Driving north, follow US 101 as it winds up through Marin County to San Rafael, the largest city in the county, where the Spanish founded a Mission in 1817.

8 miles further north turn right for Highway 37. Cross the Petaluma River then turn left at Sears Point onto Highway 121. Follow the signs into Sonoma via Highway 12, continuing to the central Plaza. Turn right by the Mission building along East Spain Street to reach the Sebastiani Winery.

2 SONOMA

The history of this third-generation, family-owned vineyard stretches back to the arrival of Samuele Sebastiani from Tuscany in 1895. A free and informative half-hour winery and tasting tour admits visitors into its pungent and shadowy world, where old world know-how meets state-of-the-art technology and the barrels come as mighty as redwood trees. A short walk west along East Spain Street brings you to Sonoma's central plaza and Mission buildings. See page 116.

Leave Sonoma via West Napa Street, traveling north along Highway 12 (signposted to Santa Rosa). Turn left for Glen Ellen, then turn right by the London Lodge for the Jack London State Historic Park.

3 JACK LONDON STATE HISTORIC PARK

On the way up you will pass the charming Benziger Winery, where visitors can try the wine and follow a self-guided tour of the vineyards. Jack London State Park was the final home of the roving, bestselling author Jack London, see page 114.

Return the same way to Highway 12. Continue north, then turn right onto Trinity Road, signposted to Oakville. This scenic drive cuts over the hills to the Napa Valley. When you reach Highway 29, turn left.

4 NAPA VALLEY

Forming a spine for the Napa Valley, Highway 29 is lined with flagship wineries built in ostentatious styles that range from pompous châteaux to post-modernist bunkers. This tour recommends starting with a picnic under the trees at the V Sattui Winery, on the right, where there is a delicatessen. Further north in St Helena, the German-origin Beringer Vineyard, on the left, dates from 1876 and exemplifies the old money Napa winery.

Continue north towards Calistoga, but turn right just before it into Dunaweal Lane. Sterling Vineyards on the right, with its 1968 whitewashed pseudo-Greek hilltop monastery reached by ski-lift, represents the upstart humor of new generation vintners. Clos Pegase, on the opposite side of the

Fruits of the Rhine: German immigrants founded the Beringer Vineyard in St Helena in 1876

road, is the winery as art temple, with a 1986 showhouse and lawns adorned with modern sculpture.

Continue along Dunaweal Lane and turn right to join the Silverado Trail, a former stagecoach route that runs south parallel to Highway 29. Follow it down to Napa, joining with Highway 121, then the Highway 29 freeway towards Vallejo. Turn right onto Highway 37.

5 SAN PABLO BAY

This route crosses the mouth of the River Napa to skirt the level shoreline of the San Pablo Bay National Wildlife Refuge.

Continue back to US 101, turning south for the Golden Gate Bridge and San Francisco.

Blame it all on the god of wine – sculpture at Clos Pegase Winery

Highway 1

This 160-mile tour winds south along Highway 1, one of the most famous coastal roads in America, to visit the seaside resort of Santa Cruz. The return route climbs inland to enjoy the redwood forests and panoramas of the Santa Cruz Mountains. If you want to laze on the beach or hike in the woods, consider spending a night in or near Santa Cruz. (For map of route see page 111.)
Allow one or two days.

This itinerary leaves San Francisco via Daly City. Follow any sign south for Interstate 280, then take the Pacifica exit to pick up Highway 1.

Half Moon Bay

1 HIGHWAY 1

The road winds south hugging the coast, passing the fragrant eucalyptus woods of the San Pedro Valley County Park and beaches and headlands that in summer can be eerily shrouded in fog. Half Moon Bay has a splendid crescent of sands, and is famous for its October Pumpkin Festival when the surrounding fields turn bright orange. Many of the towns along here were originally settled by Portuguese and Italian farmers and fishermen. A noticeable landmark is the 1872 115-foot Pigeon Point Lighthouse, which is open for visitors on Sundays and has a youth hostel in its outbuildings.
Turn right for Año Nuevo State Reserve.

2 POINT AÑO NUEVO

Whale-watching and observing breeding elephant seals are the main attractions at this coastal wildlife sanctuary. See page 121.
Continue southeast along Highway 1.

Big trees at Big Basin – one of the best spots in the Bay Area to enjoy the majesty of redwood forests

3 SANTA CRUZ

The road sweeps down past the fog-less blue Pacific to this thoroughly American seaside resort. Turn right into Bay Street, following signs to the Beach Boardwalk. See page 123.

When you leave Santa Cruz, cross Highway 1 to drive north up Highway 9.

4 BIG BASIN REDWOODS STATE PARK

The road snakes up into the shady woods and inland villages that border the River San Lorenzo. Continue climbing through the Henry Cowell Redwoods State Park to Ben Lomond and then Boulder Creek, where you might want to stop for a snack or to buy some picnic provisions. Turn left up Highway 236, passing a golf course to reach the Big Basin Redwoods State Park. (If you prefer to omit this detour, continue along Highway 9.)

With 19,000 acres of redwood forest and parkland, Big Basin is a perfect place to fall in love with trees that were mere striplings when Columbus discovered the New World. An hour-long trail guides visitors round some of its mightiest examples, including the 329-foot tall "Mother" and the 2,000-year-old "Father" of the forest.

Continue driving north through the park on Highway 236. This descends to rejoin Highway 9. Turn left following the sign for Saratoga. When you reach Skyline Boulevard (Highway 35) turn left, signposted to San Francisco.

5 SKYLINE BOULEVARD

This beautiful drive meanders north through the forests and parks of the Santa Cruz Mountains, offering alternating views west to the sea and east to the South Bay. Lonely rows of mailboxes are the only signs of life – spare time to stop at a vista point and enjoy the tranquillity.

Turn right down Highway 84, signposted to Woodside, to join the Junipero Serra freeway (Interstate 280). Continue north to San Francisco.

SILICON VALLEY

The southern end of San Francisco Bay is known as Silicon Valley, which stretches for 25 miles between Palo Alto and its capital, San Jose. A century ago this land was dappled with orchards and vineyards, but since the 1970s it has grown prosperously urban from harvesting AppleMacs and IBMs. Its nickname derives from the silicon chip, a popular term for the minuscule electronic circuits stored on a silicon crystal that power computers and many other technological wonders.

Encouraged by the presence of progressive universities like Stanford and Berkeley, hi-tech industries have been gathering in Santa Clara County since the 1950s. Today's electronics and computer empires have grown from seeds planted by young scientists like Steve Jobs and Steve Wozniak, who in 1975 set out to design a powerful computer for home and office use. They started work in Jobs' garage with funds raised by selling a Volkswagen van, calling their new-fangled invention "Apple" as it represented the cleanness and simplicity they sought. Within six years they had 4,000 employees and a billion-dollar turnover.

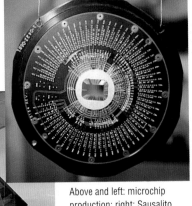

Above and left: microchip production; right: Sausalito

Today there are some 1,500 computer firms working in the Valley, and commentators inevitably liken this boom to a second Gold Rush. Ironically, the new communications and information technologies it has spawned means that businesses no longer need to be located here, and now every go-ahead nation has its own Silicon Strip, Coast or Valley.

GETTING AWAY FROM IT ALL

"I'm sittin' on the dock of the Bay,
Watching the tide roll away."
OTIS REDDING,
1967

Getting Away from It All

*E*veryone knows that green hills, sandy beaches and outdoor adventures are just a short drive or ferry ride away from San Francisco. What's remarkable is that they can all be found within the city too.

BALLOONING
Balloons Above the Valley
Day and sunset flights over Napa Valley.
5091 St Helena Highway, Napa.
Tel: 707/253–2222.

Once in a Lifetime
Flights over Sonoma Valley from winery sites.
Tel: 707/578–0580.

CYCLING
The mountain bike was invented on the slopes of Mount Tamalpais, and San Francisco has much to offer the cyclist who doesn't mind the odd climb. You could follow part of the 49-Mile Scenic Drive (see page 106), and on Sundays, when John F Kennedy Drive is closed, Golden Gate Park offers 7.5 miles of cycling. For a ride across Golden Gate Bridge, see page 104. Bicycles can be taken on ferries and BART – rental shops can suggest routes. Ring first to check availability and what deposit is required.

American Rentals
2715 Hyde Street (near Fisherman's Wharf). Tel: 415/931–0234.

Start to Finish
2530 Lombard Street. Tel: 415/202–9830.

HIKING
There is a rich choice of trails in and around San Francisco. The Marin Headlands, Mount Tamalpais, Angel Island and all parts of the Golden Gate National Recreation Area are popular tramping grounds (see individual entries). Visitor Centers can provide routes and maps, and bookstores sell specialist guides.

HORSERIDING
See page 156.

SCENIC FLIGHTS
Taking to the skies is an unbeatable way to see the city and the Bay; most companies provide a door-to-door service.

San Francisco Seaplane Tours
Seaplane flights over the Bay and city from Pier 39 or Sausalito.
Tel: 415/332–4843.

Heli USA
Helicopter flights over the city and Bay from a heliport in Sausalito.
Tel: 1–800/443–5487.

Scenic Air Tours
Spectacular flights over the city in high-wing Cessna aircraft. Complimentary pick-up.
Tel: 1–800/957–2364.

WHALEWATCHING
Oceanic Society Expeditions
High season is December to April, when grey whales migrating between Alaska and Mexico pass by.
Fort Mason Center, Building E.
Tel: 415/474–3385.

Bay Aero Tours
Whalewatching from the air.
Tel: 415/207–0044.

BEACHES
San Francisco lacks the beaches and
seaside culture of southern California,
but there are still plenty of sands and
rolling Pacific waves to enjoy in the city
and nearby.

Baker Beach
On the southwest side of the Presidio,
this is the most popular beach in city
limits. The sea is cold and unsafe for
swimming, but its sands are enjoyed by
walkers and sunbathers – nude at the
northern end.
*Take Bowley Street then Gibson Road west
from Lincoln Boulevard. Bus: 29.*

China Beach
This small pocket of sand in the Seacliff
district gets its name from the Chinese
fishing junks that once anchored here.
Swimming is safe, with lifeguards on
duty in the summer.
North of Seacliff Avenue. Bus: 29.

Drake's Beach
See page 137.

Ocean Beach
Kite-fliers, jilted lovers, joggers, film-
makers, fog addicts, surf heroes – Ocean
Beach, with four miles of wind-ravaged
sands running down the west side of the
city from Cliff House to Fort Funston,
will please anyone except swimmers as
the strong currents make bathing unsafe.
*By Great Highway. Metro: L, N. Bus: 5,
31, 38, 71.*

Stinson Beach
Complement a visit to Muir Woods or
Mount Tamalpais State Park (see pages
115 and 136) with a trip to San
Francisco's best beach – a three-mile
sandbar where swimming is safe and
sheltered. There are picnic facilities,
lifeguards in summer and plenty of
people to watch.
*20 miles northwest via Highway 1. Open:
daily 9am–6pm. Parking charge. Road and
weather information, tel: 415/868–1922.
Bus: Golden Gate Transit at weekends.*

Surfing at Fort Point – San Francisco's
waters are often cold and rough

BOAT TRIPS

You won't have "done" San Francisco till you've had a spin on the Bay. Services are geared to suit both commuters and visitors, and depart from either Fisherman's Wharf or the Ferry Building. Call to check times before setting out.

Blue & Gold Fleet

Regular ferry services to Oakland and Alameda, Bay cruises. Departures from Ferry Building or Pier 39.
Pier 39, Fisherman's Wharf.
Tel: 415/705–5444.

Golden Gate Ferries

Regular ferry services to Sausalito and Larkspur departing from the south end of the Ferry Building.
Ferry Building, Embarcadero and Market Street. Tel: 415/932–2000.

Red & White Fleet

Regular ferry services to Sausalito, Tiburon and Vallejo. Tours of Alcatraz and Angel Island, Bay cruises. Departures from Pier 41, Pier 43½ or Ferry Building.
Pier 41, Fisherman's Wharf. Tel: 415/546–2628. Credit card booking, tel: 415/546–2700.

CITY PARKS

Don't think Golden Gate Park and the Presidio (see pages 60 and 81) are the only green spaces in San Francisco.

Aquatic Park

See page 37.

Crissy Field

On the northern shore of the Presidio, Crissy Field was established as a military airfield in 1919 and played a pioneering rôle in early American aviation. Now part of the Golden Gate National Recreation Area, it is a peaceful, often windy, open space. The adjacent waters are popular with experienced windsurfers.
Mason Street. Bus: 29.

Lake Merced

In the southwest corner of the city, this natural lake is mainly used for boating, trout fishing and relaxation in the surrounding parkland.
By Lake Merced Boulevard. Bus: 18.

Lincoln Park

A green frame for the California Palace of the Legion of Honor (see page 40), Lincoln Park used to be the site of San Francisco's municipal cemetery before

A trip across the Bay is an essential part of any visit to San Francisco – and great fun

this was re-sited in 1909 to the south of the city at Colma in San Mateo County. The 270-acre area was landscaped by John McLaren, the designer of Golden Gate Park, and today incorporates an 18-hole public golf course and several walking trails.

Main entrance at Clement Street and 34th Avenue. Bus: 18, 38.

Marina Green

This strip of green between Fort Mason and the Presidio stages a free daily display of the self-punishing sports and fitness regimes that are apparently crucial to the survival of many San Franciscans. You may think you've stumbled on a city marathon, but in fact it's just the regular tide of after-work, Walkman-carrying joggers pounding the shoreline.

This area was developed for the 1915 Panama-Pacific International Exposition, and now has a marina and the private St Francis Yacht Club. At the far eastern end of the adjacent West Harbor Jetty is a Wave Organ developed by workers from the Exploratorium with some 20 pipes playing liquid music.

By Marina Boulevard. Bus: 22, 30.

Sigmund Stern Memorial Grove

A 63-acre wooded park in the sedate southwest of the city, worth visiting mainly for the free concerts staged in its natural amphitheater on Sunday afternoons in the summer.

By 19th Avenue and Sloat Boulevard. Metro: K, M. Bus: 23, 28.

Lake Merced – a park for fishing and dreaming

Sutro Heights Park

Overlooking the north end of Ocean Beach, this park was originally the mansion and enthusiastically nurtured grounds of the property magnate Adolph Sutro. After his family left in 1938 the house fell into ruins and was eventually demolished. Since 1976 its gardens have been part of the Golden Gate National Recreation Area – now a strange and forgotten, often fog-bound, cliff-top sanctuary.

At the west end of Point Lobos Avenue. Bus: 38, 38L.

GOLDEN GATE NATIONAL RECREATION AREA

Many of the green splashes on the San Francisco map belong to the 80,000-acre Golden Gate National Recreation Area (GGNRA), the most visited national park in the United States. Established in 1972, its protected lands stretch south from Point Reyes Station to Sweeney Ridge, and include historic attractions such as Alcatraz, the Presidio and the San Francisco Maritime National Historic Park. Most of the city's northern and western shoreline falls under its jurisdiction including Fort Mason, Crissy Field, Ocean Beach and Fort Funston. North of the Golden Gate Bridge, the GGNRA's realm includes the Marin Headlands, Muir Woods and Stinson Beach.

To get the best of GGNRA, buy a copy of the official *Park Guide* which includes maps and trail information. Free or inexpensive literature with information on walks, biking and horseriding trails, wildlife, recreational facilities and picnic spots is also available from Visitor Centers at main sites. A free quarterly calendar of what's on information, *Park Events*, lists the detailed program of events in the park, which vary from a backcountry mountain-bike ride to a peek around the Presidio Cemetery. Information is also available from GGNRA Park Headquarters, Building 201, Fort Mason Center (see page 56).
GGNRA Information, tel: 415/556–0560. Parkcast (weather information), tel: 415/556–6030.

Golden Gate Promenade

This four-mile walk runs along San Francisco's northern shoreline from Aquatic Park to Fort Point, offering fine views of Golden Gate Bridge and plenty of stress-defusing sea air.

Fort Funston

Named after General Frederick Funston, the military commander of the Presidio at the time of the 1906 earthquake, these windy cliffs and dunes to the south of Ocean Beach are popular with hikers, horse riders and hang-gliders.
Skyline Boulevard. Ranger Office. Tel: 415/239–2366. Open: daily 8:30am–5pm. Bus: 18, 23.

Land's End

At the northern edge of Lincoln Park, these wild, shipwrecking headlands can be reached by a coastal trail running between the California Palace of the Legion of Honor and Point Lobos.
Bus: 18.

Olema Valley

Running north–south alongside Bolinas Ridge for nine miles, this pastoral valley makes a pleasant drive past sweeping fields, historic farms and orchards.
30 miles north on Highway 1. Bear Valley Visitor Center. Tel: 415/663–1092.

Sweeney Ridge

The mountain ridge from which San Francisco Bay was first seen by European eyes is now the focal point of a 1,047-acre nature park to the south of San

REDWOOD PALACES

The tallest trees in the world, coastal redwoods thrive in the cool, moist environment of the fog belts of California and Oregon. *Sequoia sempervirens* can often grow to heights of over 300 feet, though it is their inland relatives *sequoia gigantea*, the giant sequoias on the western slopes of the Sierra Nevada mountains, that have the longer lifespan and greater bulk. The trees' red bark is resistant to fire, fungus and insects, and their thick, shallow roots extend up to 100 feet to catch water condensed from the fog passing through the branches above. Walk amidst them at Muir Woods (see page 115).

Francisco. The Spanish Captain Gaspar de Portolá climbed up here on 4 November 1769 during a 10-month expedition searching for Monterey Bay. A 1.8-mile walk leads up to the Portola Discovery Site, but be aware that fog can often obscure this historic view. There are several trails to follow through scrub and grassland, and on a good day you can see the Farallon Islands, Point Reyes and Mount Diablo.
13 miles south, near San Bruno. Take Sneath Lane exit from Highway 35 (Skyline Boulevard) or Interstate 280. Tel: 415/556–8371.

Most of the city shoreline is protected by the Golden Gate National Recreation Area

Many San Franciscans like to escape to
Angel Island for a day in the country

*Tel: 415/546–2628. Angel Island Ferry
from Tiburon, tel: 415/435–2131. Park
Information. Tel: 415/435–1915.*

Farallon Islands
A cluster of small granite islands 30 miles
west of San Francisco, the Farallones are
a rocky wildlife sanctuary inhabited by
seals, sea-lions and a host of seabirds
including puffins, cormorants, guillemots
and some 25,000 gulls. Oceanic Society
Expeditions arrange escorted whale,
dolphin and birdwatching trips.
Tel: 415/474–3385.

MOUNT TAMALPAIS STATE PARK
If you like hiking, Mount Tam is the
perfect host. Rising to 2,571 feet, it has
over 200 miles of trails to suit all abilities
and vista requirements – including one
from Panoramic Highway down to Muir
Woods and a path following what used
to be the world's crookedest railway line.
The park covers 6,400 acres, picnic and
camping sites and a Mountain Theater.
Information can be picked up at the Pan
Toll Ranger Station on Panoramic
Highway. Access to the summit may be
restricted if there is a fire hazard.
*15 miles north via Highway 1 and
Panoramic Highway. Tel: 415/388–2070.
Admission charge for vehicles.*

POINT REYES NATIONAL SEASHORE
For a sense of the natural peace, space
and bounty that must have filled the
hearts of the first Europeans to visit the
Bay Area, head for this 67,000-acre
protected coastline. Information is
available from the Bear Valley Visitor

ISLANDS

Angel Island State Park
Now a peaceful State Park that looms
over the bustle of the Bay, 740-acre
Angel Island was once the Pacific
equivalent of New York's Ellis Island.
From 1910 to 1940 an immigration
station here processed refugees and
would-be settlers from Asia and
elsewhere, including around 175,000
Chinese. Remnants of this and military
garrisons built in the second half of the
19th century survive on the island.

Angel Island is the largest island in
the Bay and has a Visitor Center, picnic
sites and 12 miles of roads and hiking
trails winding up to its 776-foot high
summit, Mount Livermore. Take a
bicycle and a picnic and have a lazy day.
Ferry: Red & White from Pier 43½.

Center, a short drive west of Olema. Point Reyes National Seashore lies on the west side of the San Andreas Fault – an Earthquake Trail in the park calmly explains that you are standing in a rift between the Pacific and North American tectonic plates.

One rewarding goal here is Drake's Beach, a windswept beach 15 miles west of the Visitor Center. This is thought to be the site where the English seafarer Sir Francis Drake landed on June 17, 1579, to claim "Nova Albion" (New England) for his queen, Elizabeth I. He and his crew stayed here for five weeks, trading with the native Miwok Indians and stocking the *Golden Hind* with provisions before continuing their circumnavigation of the globe. British visitors will reflect,

as Drake surely did, on how similar this coastal landscape is to that of their homeland.

Much of the coast here is home to isolated ranches dating back to the mid-19th century. Connoisseurs of land's ends will press on to Point Reyes lighthouse, a favorite spot for whalewatching reached by a long and winding road and a 300-step descent. San Francisco may be less than a hour and half's drive away, but here you feel truly away from it all.

Visitor Center, tel: 415/663–1092. 35 miles northwest via US 101 and Sir Francis Drake Boulevard. Open access.

Point Reyes National Seashore has some of the most invigorating landscape in the Bay Area

Wildlife

Nature is never far away in San Francisco. You'll find buffalo roaming in Golden Gate Park, sea-lions sunbathing on pontoons beside Pier 39, brown pelicans posing beside Cliff House – there's even a small community of Californian salamanders living on the parade ground at Alcatraz. The Bay Area provides ready access to a great variety of wildlife habitats around the Bay, with informative leaflets and free guided tours with rangers available in most parts of the Golden Gate National Recreation Area.

The Pacific Ocean is a prime cause of local addiction to binoculars. Blue, humpback, killer and gray whales all pass by offshore in their migration along the length of America's West Coast. Every year some 15,000 gray whales make a round trip between summer feeding grounds in the Bering Straits and winter breeding grounds off Mexico, traveling 10,000 miles in less than two months. December to April is the best time to watch them.

Californian sea-lions, the larger Steller sea-lions, harbor seals and enormous elephant seals all benefit from protected marine life sanctuaries such as the Farallon Islands, Point Reyes National Seashore and Point Año Nuevo. Seabirds are also thriving from the environmental awareness of today's Bay Area residents – egg-hunters in the Gold Rush virtually wiped out the gull colonies on Alcatraz, but today nests of breeding birds are an unexpected treat for visitors to the island in June.

Inland, California's famous redwood forests offer much more than magnificent trees. Black-tailed deer, racoons, gray squirrels and chipmunks are some residents, while birdlife ranges from the beautiful blue-black Steller's jay to obscure characters with hip-hop names like towhee, junco and vireo. Hawk-lovers should head for the Marin Headlands between September and October, when at peak times over 2,000 birds a day can be seen migrating south.

Below: elephant seals at Point Año Nuevo; right: Thirties mural in Coit Tower

DIRECTORY

"I have seen purer liquors, better segars, finer tobacco, truer guns, larger Bowie knives and prettier courtesans here in San Francisco than in any other place I have visited ... California can and does furnish the best bad things obtainable in America."

Preacher HINTON HELPER, 1855

Shopping

*W*hilst most of us shop to live, many Californians seem to live to shop. Best seen as a source of public therapy, San Francisco's malls and shopping streets are full of lovely things to wander amongst, admire and maybe even buy.

WHERE TO SHOP

San Francisco's shopping heart is Union Square and its neighboring blocks. Here you will find department stores such as Macy's and Neiman Marcus, and designer shops like Emporio Armani, Tiffany and Saks Fifth Avenue. Fisherman's Wharf and Chinatown have everything a tourist needs (and plenty you don't), but the most rewarding shopping will probably result from casual finds made while visiting neighborhoods like North Beach, Union Street, Hayes Valley and Haight-Ashbury. These areas all have small shops with individual style. If you need to take presents home, museum stores, like those at SFMOMA and the California Academy of Sciences, are a good source.

OPENING HOURS

Most shops are open at least Monday to Saturday 10am–6pm, with extended hours some evenings and Sunday opening depending on their location and merchandise.

PRICES

All purchases are subject to 8.5 percent sales tax, unless goods are shipped outside the state (duty will be payable at their destination). As prices are displayed pre-tax, this invariably results in checks (bills) coming to odd amounts. Credit cards are widely accepted, as are traveler's checks. Most retailers can provide information on packaging and shipping items home.

WHAT TO BUY

Being one of the most Europhile cities in the US, San Francisco's shops are stocked with many items similar to those on sale in Europe, particularly kitchenware, stationery, youth fashion, and furniture and crafts imports from India and Asia. Good San Franciscan buys include books, particularly as so many quality authors have written about the city (see page 16), recorded music, casualwear and decorative goods for the home. Many visitors like the idea of buying a pair of Levis jeans in the city that gave them to the world, while others go for the hippy culture posters, jewelry and tie-dye shirts and other

Sports gear supporting the city's baseball and football teams are popular buys

Typical San Francisco souvenirs: miniature cable cars, bridges and Victorian houses

paraphernalia on sale in Haight Street. If you find it won't all go into the suitcase, Chinatown is a convenient source of inexpensive luggage.

MARKETS
Heart of the City Farmer's Market
Fresh fruit, vegetables and produce from the Bay Area.
United Nations Plaza, Civic Center.
Wednesday and Sunday.

Ferry Plaza Farmer's Market
Fruit, vegetables, flowers and cookery demonstrations.
By the Ferry Building, Embarcadero.
Saturday morning.

SHOPPING CENTERS
See also entries for The Cannery, Ghirardelli Square and Pier 39.

The Anchorage
Souvenir shops, restaurants and street entertainers in the heart of Fisherman's Wharf.
2800 Leavenworth Street at Jefferson Street.
Tel: 415/775–6000.

Crocker Galleria
Stylish glass-domed arcade with boutique shops, in the Financial District.
Entrances on Post and Sutter streets,
between Montgomery and Kearny streets.
Tel: 415/393–1505. See page 92–3.

Embarcadero Center
Vast three-level, eight-block office and retail complex linked by above-street walkways and incorporating the Hyatt Regency Hotel.
West of Embarcadero between Clay and
Sansome streets. Tel: 415/772–0500.

Rincon Center
Aesthetic shopping venue centered around an art deco post office with murals by the Russian-born Anton Refregier.
101 Spear Street at Mission Street.
Tel: 415/543–8600.

San Francisco Shopping Center
Over a hundred shops on nine floors, worth a visit just to ride its unique spiral escalators.
Market Street at Fifth Street.
Tel: 415/495–5656.

AMERICANA
Disney Store
All your favorite cartoon characters in infinitely purchasable form.
Pier 39, Fisherman's Wharf.
Tel: 415/391–4119.

Outlaw Harley-Davidson Specialties
Cult motorbike merchandise.
Ghirardelli Square, 900 North Point Street.
Tel: 415/563–8986.

Positively Haight Street
Hippy memorabilia and rock music T-shirts.
1157 Masonic Avenue.
Tel: 415/252–8747.

Quantity Postcards
Psst – want to buy 10,000 postcards?
1441 Grant Avenue. Tel: 415/986–8866.

White Buffalo Gallery
American Indian jewelry, belts, rugs and crafts.
Ghirardelli Square, 900 North Point Street.
Tel: 415/931–0665.

ANTIQUES
Jackson Square is the center of San Francisco's antiques trade with over 25 shops grouped together. See page 67.
455 Jackson Street. Tel: 415/296–8150.

BOOKS
Borders
Vast books and music store with café on Union Square, open to 10pm weekdays.
400 Post Street. Tel: 415/399–1633.

Maritime Store
Books on San Francisco and maritime subjects.
Hyde Street Pier, Fisherman's Wharf.
Tel: 415/775–2665.

Rand McNally Map & Travel Store
Guides, maps and travel-related books.
595 Market Street. Tel: 415/777–3131.

CHILDREN
Basic Brown Bear Factory
Everything you need to stuff, sew, bath, groom and dress your teddy.
The Cannery, 2801 Leavenworth Street.
Tel: 415/931–6670.

F A O Schwarz
The ultimate toy store for both adults and children.
48 Stockton Street. Tel: 415/394–8700.

Gap Kids
Practical street gear for Junior.
100 Post Street. Tel: 415/421–4906.

CLOTHES
Brooks Brothers
Suits, shirts and casualwear for the stylish executive.
201 Post Street. Tel: 415/397–4500.

Dinostore
Hip clothes, shoes and accessories for women, in the Haight.
1553 Haight Street. Tel: 415/861–3933.

Hats on Post
Ladies' hats for all moods.
210 Post Street. Tel: 415/392–3737.

Headlines
Levis, Ray-Bans, cowboy boots and other American essentials.
833 Market Street. Tel: 415/956–4872.

CRAFTS
Genji
Japanese antiques, furniture and crafts.
Japan Center, 1675 Post Street.
Tel: 415/931–1616.

Gump's
Fine china, glass, jewelry, Asian antiques.
250 Post Street. Tel: 415/982–1616.

DEPARTMENT STORES
Macy's
The world in a store, spread over two buildings.
Stockton and O'Farrell.
Tel: 415/397–3333.

Neiman Marcus
Upmarket clothes, jewelry and household goods, plus the top-floor Rotunda restaurant.
150 Stockton Street. Tel: 415/362–3900.

FABRIC
Britex Fabrics
Four floors of dress and furnishing fabrics.
146 Geary Street. Tel: 415/392–2910.

FACTORY OUTLETS
Six-Sixty Center
Most discount warehouses lie south of Market Street and mainly sell clothes and sportswear for women and children. Some dedication is required to track down individual outlets, but this shopping center conveniently gathers many bargain goods under one roof.
660 3rd Street. Tel: 415/227–0464.

FOOD AND DRINK
Caffè Roma Coffee Roasting Co
Aromatic North Beach café and roasting house with coffee beans and blends for sale.
526 Columbus Avenue. Tel: 415/296–7662.

Il Fornaio Bakery
Superlative Italian breads and biscuits.
2298 Union Street. Tel: 415/563–0746.

Woks for all: Chinatown is a favorite place for a wander round the shops

Napa Valley Winery Exchange
Downtown Californian wine specialists.
415 Taylor Street. Tel: 415/771–2887.

Ten Ren Tea Co
Chinese teas and herbs.
949 Grant Avenue. Tel: 415/362–0656.

FOR THE HOME
Fillamento
Designer crockery, cutlery and household treats.
2185 Fillmore Street. Tel: 415/931–2224.

The Wok Shop
Everything you need to be a *dim-sum* wizard back home.
718 Grant Avenue. Tel: 415/989–3797.

Williams-Sonoma
Kitchenware shop with gourmet gifts and goodies.
150 Post Street. Tel: 415/362–6904.

MUSIC
Tower Records
Music emporium by Columbus Avenue, open daily till midnight.
2568 Jones Street. Tel: 415/441–4880.

Entertainment

*F*rom the Gold Rush days of saloons, whorehouses and gambling dens, to the hi-tech concert halls and hip dance clubs of today, San Francisco has always been a good time city.

WHAT'S ON

San Francisco's two daily newspapers, *The Chronicle* and *The Examiner*, carry listings of mainstream cultural events in the city. A bumper compendium, known locally as "The Pink Pages" but called *Datebook*, comes out on Sundays. The free *Arts Monthly* is a calendar of visual and performing arts events. The *Bay Guardian* and *SF Weekly*, both free weekly papers, are the best source for alternative entertainment and nightlife.

Events Line

24-hour recorded information compiled by the San Francisco Convention and Visitors Bureau.
Tel: 415/391–2001.

TICKETS
BASS Tickets

BASS (Bay Area Seating Service) has several outlets around the city. Most people buy through BASS because there is no satisfactory alternative. A facility charge is levied on each ticket.
Information and credit card bookings, tel: 510/762–2277.

Mr Ticket

Best seats for top arts and sports events at prices above face value.
2065 Van Ness Avenue.
Tel: 415/775–3031.

TIX Bay Area

Half-price tickets for performances that day of selected theatre, dance and music events are available to personal callers. Payment in cash or traveler's checks only for half-price tickets. Advance bookings by credit card.
In Union Square on the Stockton Street side. Tel: 415/433–7827. Open: Tuesday to Saturday 11am–6pm (7pm Friday and Saturday). Closed: Monday, Tuesday.

BALLET

The world class San Francisco Ballet company stages a regular season of both classical ballet and new work at the War Memorial Opera House in the Civic Center between February and May. The *Nutcracker* is spectacularly staged several times during the Christmas holidays.
301 Van Ness Avenue. Tel: 415/865–2000.

CINEMAS

Going to the movies is particularly enjoyable in San Francisco because the city has several atmospheric old movie palaces, such as the Castro. The healthy choice of art and foreign films in their repertoire suggests that there really is life after Schwarzenegger. The other good news is that San Franciscans are fond of film festivals. The San Francisco Film Festival held each April/May is the oldest in the United States. The Lesbian and Gay Festival screened every June is the largest of its kind.

Most of the city's more than 50 cinemas can be found on Geary Boulevard, Clement Street, Union Street, Fillmore Street, and Van Ness Avenue.

Castro
1924 movie palace with ascending Wurlitzer organ.
429 Castro Street. Tel: 415/621–6120.

Galaxy
Multi-screen complex with new releases.
Sutter Street and Van Ness Avenue. Tel: 415/474–8700.

Kabuki 8
Eight screens showing something for everyone.
Japan Center, Post and Fillmore streets. Tel: 415/931–9800.

Red Vic
Cult hits and forgotten classics in the laid-back Haight.
1727 Haight Street. Tel: 415/668–3994.

COMEDY AND CABARET
Cobb's Comedy Club
Alternative comics – brilliant, excruciating, but always entertaining.
The Cannery, 2801 Leavenworth Street. Tel: 415/928–4320.

Finocchio's
Historic North Beach revue with female impersonators.
506 Broadway. Tel: 415/982–9388. Open: Wednesday to Sunday.

Comedians grab the stage at Cobb's Comedy Club in The Cannery

Great American Music Hall
Ornate 1907 venue with live music, comics and food.
859 O'Farrell Street. Tel: 415/885–0750.

Josie's Cabaret and Juice Joint
Castro nightspot starring gay and lesbian performers.
3583 16th Street. Tel: 415/861–7933.

DANCE VENUES
Modern, classical and ethnic dance companies frequently perform at mixed-event venues around the city. See local press for who is in town.

Cowell Theater
Pier 2, Fort Mason Center. Tel: 415/441–5706.

New Performance Gallery
3153 17th Street. Tel: 415/863–9834.

Theater Artaud
450 Florida Street. Tel: 415/621–7797.

Palace of Fine Arts
Bay and Lyon streets. Tel: 415/567–6642.

CONCERTS AND CLASSICAL MUSIC

Audium
An only-in-California theater of sound-sculptured space.
1616 Bush Street. Tel: 415/771–1616.
Friday and Saturday.

Center for the Arts Theater
Contemporary music performances.
700 Howard Street at Third Street.
Tel: 415/978–2787.

Golden Gate Park Band
Sunday afternoon concerts in the Music Concourse in Golden Gate Park.
Between California Academy of Sciences and M H de Young Memorial Museum.
Tel: 415/666–7017.

Grace Cathedral
A regular venue for concerts and choral performances, see page 62.

Old St Mary's Church
Lunchtime concerts are held every week in this Chinatown church, see page 94.
660 California Street. Tel: 415/288–3800.
Tuesdays at 12.30pm. Free.

San Francisco Symphony
This renowned orchestra plays a regular season at the Louise M Davies Symphony Hall between September and June.
In the Civic Center at Van Ness Avenue and Grove Street. Tel: 415/431–5400.

NIGHTCLUBS AND LIVE MUSIC

Harry Denton's
Trendy supper club by the Embarcadero.
161 Steuart Street. Tel: 415/882–1333.

Hornblower Dining Yachts
Dine and dance as you cruise the Bay.
Pier 33, Embarcadero. Tel: 415/788–8866.

Fillmore Auditorium
Legendary rock venue rocks on.
1805 Geary Avenue. Tel: 415/346–6000.

Johnny Love's
Live music, beautiful Californians.
1500 Broadway at Polk Street.
Tel: 415/931–8021.

Lou's Pier 47 Club
Jazz, blues and funky sounds day and night on Fisherman's Wharf.
300 Jefferson Street. Tel: 415/771–0377.

Mexican Bus
Go club-hopping by bus to Latin and Caribbean rhythms.
Friday and Saturday night.
Tel: 415/546–3747.

New Orleans Room
Quality jazz at the luxury Fairmont Hotel on Nob Hill.
950 Mason Street. Tel: 415/772–5259.

FREE SPEECH
San Franciscans' long-running love affair with books, coffee and self-expression is borne out by the many Spoken Word events held around the city. Most are free and take place in the evening – museums stage lectures, bookstores arrange readings by poets and writers, but the most intriguing events are the "open mike" evenings held in coffee bars. Anyone can sign up to read from their literary masterpiece, so expect to hear anything from a moving love poem to a transvestite's tale about trapped spiders or a student's favorite cake recipe. Look in the *Bay Guardian* for venues and times.

Paradise Lounge
Bands, bars and pool tables.
1501 Folsom Street.
Tel: 415/861–6906.

Three Babes and a Bus
Get on board the party bus for a
nightclub tour without line or
transportation worries.
Friday and Saturday night.
Tel: 415/552–2582.

Slim's
Top bands, dancing and food in
SoMa.
133 11th Street. Tel: 415/621–3330.

OPERA
The prestigious San Francisco Opera
attracts top name performers for its
regular season from September to
December at the War Memorial
Opera House.
In the Civic Center at Van Ness Avenue
and Grove Street. Tel: 415/864–3330.

THEATER
American Conservatory Theater
Classic and contemporary repertory
drama. Season runs October to June.
Stage Door Theater, 420 Mason Street.
Tel: 415/749–2228. ACT will return to its
traditional base in the Geary Theater,
Geary Street, after the building's seismic
renovation.

Asian-American Theater
New plays, sketches and workshop
productions.
403 Arguello Boulevard.
Tel: 415/751–2600.

Curran Theater
Broadway musicals and stage hits.
445 Geary Street. Tel: 415/474–3800.

Nightclub on Broadway, North Beach

Club Fugazi
Beach Blanket Babylon – a long-
running revue with topical gags, silly
costumes and celebrity spoofs, staged
in a former 1912 North Beach
community hall.
678 Green Street. Tel: 415/421–4222.

Golden Gate Theater
Musicals and stage hits.
1 Taylor Street. Tel: 415/474–3800.

Magic Theater
New plays and new writers. Season
runs October to July.
Fort Mason Center, Building D.
Tel: 415/441–8822.

Dirty Harry (above);
Basic Instinct (left);
Vertigo (right);
Bullitt (bottom right)

San Francisco is only 387 miles north of Hollywood, the Los Angeles suburb that has been the center of the US film-making industry since 1911. If the script required a cityscape, San Francisco invariably stepped into the role. In the course of this century it has matured into a venerable screen-star, inspiring many famous directors and providing spectacular backdrops for everything from *film noir* thrillers to TV commercials.

One satisfaction of watching old movies starring San Francisco is how instantly recognizable the city is. Cable cars, the skyscrapers of the Financial District, Alcatraz, the Golden Gate and Bay Bridges – all seem as potent in scratchy black and white as they do in living color. In particular, 1940s crime films such as *The Maltese Falcon* and *Dark Passage*, both starring Humphrey Bogart, and Alfred Hitchcock's 1958 *Vertigo,* have left an ominous mood hanging in its streets.

The notorious prison on Alcatraz

Starring San Francisco

has inspired an entire miniseries that includes Burt Lancaster's *Bird Man of Alcatraz* (1962), Clint Eastwood's *Escape from Alcatraz* (1979) and the recent *Murder in the First*. Chinatown became a particularly popular location in the 1980s, appearing in films like *Hammett*, *Dim Sum* and *The Dead Pool*, and other notable films exploiting areas of the

city include *Presidio*, *Pacific Heights* and *Bullitt*, which used its switchback hills to create the ultimate city car chase.

Today San Francisco is known as "North Hollywood," partly because barely a month goes by without a movie being shot here, but also because it has become a creative center for the film industry in its own right. The director and producer Francis Ford Coppola has his offices on Columbus Avenue, and north of the city near San Rafael the director George Lucas, creator of *Star Wars* and the Indiana Jones films, has set up a studio in Lucas Valley. Clearly, San Francisco is one actor that will never be out of work.

Annual Events

JANUARY/FEBRUARY

San Francisco's annual conga of ethnic festivals kicks off with the celebrations for **Chinese New Year** – dates vary according to the lunar calendar. The main events take place in a Chinatown ablaze with firecrackers and Good Luck banners, and include the Miss Chinatown USA beauty contest and a Golden Dragon Parade on the final Saturday night.

MARCH

Irish roots are honored on **St Patrick's Day** with church services, a good drink and a big flag-waving parade along Market Street on March 17 or the nearest Sunday. Though not an official government holiday, **Easter** is celebrated by many San Franciscans. The **Bay Area Music Awards** ("Bammies") pay tribute to local musicians.

APRIL

San Francisco's Japanese community holds its **Cherry Blossom Festival** in the latter half of the month, with performances by artists from the mother country and a parade staged in Japantown. The **San Francisco International Film Festival,** the oldest in North America, invades the city's cinemas.

MAY

On May 5 **Cinco de Mayo** remembers the Mexican victory at La Puebla in 1862 over the French. Festivities are

held on the nearest weekend and culminate with the crowning of a fiesta queen in the Civic Center. At the end of the month the Mission district lets rip with a Rio-style **Carnaval** featuring costumed parades, Latin sounds and crafts and food stalls. The **Bay to Breakers** race sees costumed crowds running between the Bay and Ocean Beach.

JUNE

The last Sunday finds the **Gay and Lesbian Freedom Day Parade** whistling and waving its way down a Market Street lined with rainbow flags. **Gay Pride Week** and the **San Francisco International Lesbian and Gay Film Festival** is also held this month. Neighborhood street fairs take place in Union Street, Haight Street and North Beach.

JULY

The **Fourth of July**, Independence Day, is marked with a public holiday and fireworks galore by Crissy Field and on Golden Gate Bridge. Cable Car Bell-Ringing Championship in Union Square, Polk Street Fair.

AUGUST/SEPTEMBER

August is a quiet month save for the **Japantown Street Fair**. In September the **San Francisco Fair** takes place in the Civic Center and there are other fairs in Folsom Street and Castro Street. On the last weekend the **San Francisco Blues Festival** is staged by Fort Mason.

OCTOBER

October 12 is **Columbus Day**,

commemorating the Genoan explorer's discovery of the New World in 1492, and celebrated in style by the Italian community in North Beach. Traditional festivies include services in the Church of Saints Peter and Paul in Washington Square and a parade to Fisherman's Wharf for the blessing of the fishing fleet. **Halloween** in San Francisco is a big excuse to party – pumpkins are turned into lanterns and pies, office workers dress up in fantasy costumes, and exhibitionists let it all hang out at the Exotic Erotic Ball.

NOVEMBER

On November 2 the Mexican community remembers the **Dia de los Muertos** (Day of the Dead), when the spirits of their ancestors return, with a nocturnal procession in the Mission. The **San Francisco Jazz Festival** normally takes place in the first fortnight. On the fourth Thursday of the month, the **Thanksgiving** holiday commemorates the Pilgrim Fathers' first harvest in Massachusetts in 1621, and serves as an unofficial cue for San Franciscans to begin their Christmas shopping.

DECEMBER

Christmas in San Francisco is celebrated with elaborate displays in department store windows, Christmas caroling, performances of *The Nutcracker* by the San Francisco Ballet and a feast of present-buying and family gatherings. As in all good party towns, **New Year's Eve** is a cause of midnight madness followed by a citywide hangover the next day, which is a necessary public holiday.

Dates of some events change year to year. Contact the San Francisco Visitor Information Center for exact details.

The Chinese New Year Parade in Chinatown marks the start of a year of colorful festivities

Children

*W*ith its Big City feel and abundant parks, beaches and amusements, San Francisco is ideal for a family vacation. Along with its well-publicized cable cars, ferries and waterfront attractions, there are stimulating museums and unique historical sights to make this a memorable city for children to visit.

BABYSITTING

Hotels can usually arrange babysitting services.

Bay Area Babysitters

Established agency with experienced babysitters.
Tel: 415/991-7474.

BEACHES

See page 131.

ESSENTIALS

Parents bringing children or babies to San Francisco have little to worry about. The high standard of living in California means that all necessary supplies and medical services are to hand, including diapers, baby food and formula. If you need to rent a car seat for a child, double check availability when making the reservation. Strollers can be rented from some bike rental shops, such as American Rentals, see page 130. For 24-hour pharmacies see page 183.

HOTELS

In their competitive attempt to be "family friendly," many hotels have introduced elaborate children's programs. These can range from enrollment in a Kids' Club to the provision of child-size dressing gowns, and – at the Clift Hotel – the installation of a miniature piano for your budding Mozart. Before making a reservation, always ask how a hotel plans to make your darling(s) feel at home.

MUSEUMS

San Francisco enjoys an abundance of museums. Those of particular appeal to the young are the California Academy of Sciences, with its Discovery Room, Tactile Dome, Planetarium and marine life, and the Exploratorium, a hands-on science lab. See pages 39 and 52 respectively. Age limits vary between museums for free or discounted admission for children.

Public playground in the Civic Center – San Francisco really is a great place for kids!

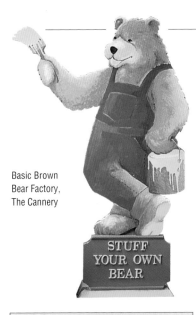

Basic Brown
Bear Factory,
The Cannery

WHAT NOW?
San Francisco

Around the Bay

Bay Area Discovery Museum
Adventure museum with arts, performance and science activities, including a San Francisco Bay hall where children can steer a fishing boat and crawl through an undersea tunnel. There is a café, picnic area and fine views of the Golden Gate Bridge – allow half a day. *On the north side of Golden Gate Bridge, take the Alexander Avenue exit. Building 557, East Fort Baker. Tel: 415/332–7674. Open: Tuesday to Sunday 10am–5pm from 15 June to 15 September, rest of year Wednesday to Sunday 10am–5pm. Closed: Monday, Tuesday in winter. Admission charge but free first Thursday of month.*

PLAYGROUNDS
Founded in 1888, the children's playground in Golden Gate Park is the oldest in America in a public park. There are others in Washington Square (North Beach), Portsmouth Square and Yerba Buena Gardens (see individual entries).

The Jungle
Fifteen thousand square feet of indoor adventure.
555 9th Street, Suite B3 (SoMa). Tel: 415/552–4386. Open: Monday to Thursday 9am–7pm (9pm Friday, Saturday), Sunday 10am–6pm. Admission charge.

RESTAURANTS
Fast food outlets mean that hunger pangs are easily satiated, and there are many family-orientated restaurants with highchairs, child portions and even table-top amusements. Shun the ageist few with signs saying "No Cry Babies."

TRANSPORT
On MUNI and BART under-fives travel free. Discount fares apply for ages 5 to under 17.

Sports

*W*hether you like to play or watch, sports are a great way to enjoy your stay in San Francisco.

FOOTBALL

The San Francisco 49ers are the only team to have won the Superbowl five times – the most recent was in 1995. Home games are played on Sunday afternoons between September and December at Candlestick Park. Their popularity means that getting tickets for big games can be difficult.

8 miles south on Highway 101. Tel: 408/562–4949. Ticket information, tel: 415/468–2249. Games normally start at 1pm. A special MUNI bus service operates on game days.

CANDLESTICK PARK

Built in 1960, the city's premier sporting venue can hold 60,000 spectators and is notoriously chilly. It is shared by the San Francisco's 49ers football team and the Giants baseball team. A baseball game was in progress between the Giants and the Oakland A's when the Loma Prieta earthquake struck on October 17, 1989 – one reason why there were relatively few casualties. As one reporter quipped, "this was the first time a stadium, not the fans, did The Wave."

BASEBALL

The San Francisco Giants are in the National League and play home games between April and October at 3Com (Candlestick) Park.
8 miles south on Highway 101. General information, tel: 415/467–8000. BASS Tickets, tel: 510/762–2277.

The Oakland Athletics (the A's) are one of America's most successful baseball teams and are in the American League. Home games are played at the Oakland Coliseum.
66th Avenue and Hegenberger Road (off Interstate 880). BART: Coliseum. Tel: 510/638–0500.

BASKETBALL

The NBA Golden State Warriors play at the Oakland Coliseum Arena.
66th Avenue and Hegenberger Road (off Interstate 880). BART: Coliseum. BASS Tickets, tel: 510/762–2277.

CYCLING

See page 130.

FISHING

Lake Merced Boating and Fishing

Licences and rod rental for fishing for trout, bass and catfish in Lake Merced.
1 Harding Road, Lake Merced. Tel: 415/753–1101.

Candlestick Park is San Francisco's main sporting arena

Sea fishing

Take a wander around the sports fishing boats moored in Jefferson Lagoon, Fisherman's Wharf, to find out what trips are on offer according to the season. Expeditions leave very early in the morning and take the best part of the day, with add-on prices for rod rental, day licence and equipment. Salmon, bass and halibut are the most likely catch.
Captain Bob, tel: 415/564–2706.

FITNESS CENTERS

Major business-orientated hotels often have their own gym and fitness facilities, or an arrangement enabling guests to use those of a nearby club. They will also have suggested jogging routes in the immediate area.

Club One

Comprehensive fitness facilities and classes.
350 Third Street. Tel: 415/512–1010.

GOLF

San Francisco has three public golf courses in the city, and there are many more private ones in the Bay Area.

Golden Gate Park

Nine holes.
47th Avenue and Fulton Street. Tel: 415/751–8987.

Harding Park

Eighteen holes.
Harding Road near Skyline Boulevard. Tel: 415/664–4690.

Lincoln Park

Eighteen holes.
34th Avenue and Clement Street. Tel: 415/221–9911.

HORSERACING
Bay Meadows Race Track
Thoroughbred horse races are held between August and January at this San Mateo course. Daily races from Wednesday to Sunday and on holiday Mondays. Night races are held on Fridays.
2600 South Delaware Street (off US 101 at Highway 92). Tel: 415/574–7223.

HORSEBACK RIDING
Golden Gate Park Stables
Tour the park on horseback. Short rides, instruction and children's ponies are available.
John F Kennedy Drive and 36th Avenue. Tel: 415/668–7360. Open: Tuesday to Sunday 8am–5pm. Closed: Monday. Reservations required.

Miwok Stables
Enjoy the Marin Headlands on horseback.
Tennessee Valley, Marin Headlands. Tel: 415/383–8048.

Sea Horse Ranch
Ride the beaches of Half Moon Bay.
1828 Cabrillo Highway. Tel: 415/726–2362.

KAYAKING
Sea Trek Ocean Kayaking Center
Escorted half- and full-day trips along San Francisco and Sausalito waterfronts in single or double kayaks. Departures from Schoonmaker Point Marina, Sausalito.
PO Box 561, Woodacre. Tel: 415/488–1000.

RACETRACKS
The nearest racetrack is **Sears Point International Raceway** at the southern end of the Sonoma Valley. Motor sports events take place every weekend.
At the junction of Highways 37 and 121. Tel: 1–800/870–8448.

ROLLER-SKATING
Roller-skaters and roller-bladers are dynamic features of San Francisco's streets and parks. If you want to join this urban disco, boots and protective gear can be rented from vans beside Ocean Beach and from specialist shops.

Skates On/Off Haight
Skate rentals and lessons.
1818 Haight Street. Tel: 415/752–8376.

RUNNING
San Francisco hosts many events intended to make running seem like communal fun rather than a self-punishing chore. The Bay to Breakers Foot Race, held in late May, is a costumed fun run from the Embarcadero to Ocean Beach via Golden Gate Park that attracts thousands of entrants. The more serious San Francisco Marathon takes place in late July and starts on Golden Gate Bridge. Other runs include Run to the Far Side in Golden Gate Park in November and an alcohol-free midnight run in Crissy Field on New Year's Eve.

If you like to go jogging, the Golden Gate Promenade is a scenic shoreline route, and Golden Gate Park is another popular venue.

SAILING
The yachting season traditionally starts with a splendid taking to the waters at the end of April. The best way to investigate boat rental or joining a sailing trip is to visit the marinas at South Beach Harbor and across in Sausalito.

**Adventure Cat
Sailing Charters**
Career around
Alcatraz, Angel
Island and
Sausalito on a
sailing catamaran.
*Pier 40, South
Beach Marina. Tel:
415/777–1630.*

**Cass Charters
and Sailing
School**
Sailing tuition and
instruction.
*1702 Bridgeway, Sausalito.
Tel: 415/332–6789.*

Sailing round the Bay; an enjoyable pastime

**Rendezvous Charters/Spinnaker
Sailing**
Sailing boats of all sizes with or without
skipper.
*Pier 40, South Beach Marina.
Tel: 415/543–7333.*

SPAS
The Hot Tubs
Individual rooms with saunas and tubs.
*2200 Van Ness Avenue.
Tel: 415/441–8827.*

Kabuki Hot Spring
Japanese spa with shiatsu massage.
*1750 Geary Boulevard.
Tel: 415/922–6000.*

SWIMMING
Beware! The waters around San
Francisco are often cold, with strong
currents making swimming unsafe. If you
want a dip, the best place in the city is
China Beach, or drive north to Stinson
Beach (see page 131). Aquatic Park is
another swimming spot regularly used by
locals. Public swimming pools are
administered by the San Francisco
Recreation and Parks Department.
*Swimming information, tel:
415/753–7026.*

TENNIS
The San Francisco Recreation and Parks
Department provides over 100 tennis
courts around the city for free use on a
first-come basis. Ask at your hotel for the
nearest courts.
Tennis information, tel: 415/753–7032.

Golden Gate Park
Twenty-one tennis courts are available in
Golden Gate Park for a small fee. These
can be reserved at weekends.
Tel: 415/753–7101.

San Francisco Tennis Club
Private tennis facilities in SoMa.
645 Fifth Street. Tel: 415/777–9000.

WINDSURFING
San Francisco School of Windsurfing
Lessons on Lake Merced with all
equipment provided.
Tel: 415/753–3235.

Food and Drink

*D*itch the diet. Load the wallet. Summon the taste buds. You're in San Francisco, the goateed, white tunicked ambassador of regional California and diverse ethnic cuisines, where eating out is a passion and restaurants attract a level of impetuous talent and client fanaticism normally reserved for the world of high fashion.

CALIFORNIA'S CUISINE

The word most food critics reach for when asked to describe California's cuisine is "eclectic." Like the region itself, culinary enterprise here is a willfully progressive fusion of past, present and foreign styles. Classic French, new Asian, modern British, Mom's apple pie – if it tastes thrilling, who cares about titles?

The Bay Area's gastronomic reputation dates from the late 1970s, when chefs fell into step with a growing desire for healthy yet sensation-rich living. Inspired by foreign travel and the state's diverse and abundant produce, they took to using ultra-fresh ingredients to create dishes that would startle the palate, delight the eye – and please the nutritionist.

The result is a foodie heaven, featuring iconoclastic celebrity chefs, see-it-all restaurants resembling the Devil's kitchen, *nouvelle cuisine* portions on art school crockery, waiters as mellifluous as sycophantic courtiers, menus that read like multilingual crossword clues – and damn good food in a fun atmosphere. San Francisco loves all this – if you want to know a good place to eat, just find half an hour, a comfortable seat, and a San Franciscan.

DINING ETHNIC

San Francisco really does offer the world on a plate. Few tourists leave without a meal in its two busiest dining venues, Chinatown and oh-so-Italian North Beach, but the possibilities seem only limited by one's capacity for research. Russian, Japanese, Cambodian, Korean, Mesopotamian, Moroccan, Ethiopian, Indian, Mexican, Greek and Swedish are some of the tastes that await the global gourmet.

Hungry? Fisherman's Wharf is the place to go for seafood

WHAT TO EAT AND WHEN

The possibilities are dazzling – in San Francisco even the theoretically simple task of ordering a sandwich turns to a brain-damaging multiple choice interrogation.

To do things properly, breakfast should either be taken in a diner with an all-American combo of eggs, bacon, hash browns, and buttered toast with jelly, or in a Mediterranean-style café with a much considered coffee, croissants and wondering thoughts about love. Sunday means the mighty *San Francisco Chronicle-Examiner* double issue and brunch (where breakfast blends with lunch, or atrophies to a Bloody Mary).

Lunch menus are lighter and cheaper than those for dinner, and there is a relentless supply of take-aways, fast-food and 24-hour delis to fill in the gaps. San Francisco's grander hotels have recently acquired a taste for afternoon tea, served *à l'anglais* with Earl Grey, scones and bone china. Don't forget your repartee.

Dine your way around the world; Mexican *taqueria* in the Haight

Sourdough bread is a San Francisco speciality

SAN FRANCISCAN SPECIALITIES

All visitors racing over the Golden Gate Bridge are assumed to be panting to try Dungeness crab and sourdough bread. The crabs are harvested in the Bay between mid-November and June and sold in stalls and restaurants on Fisherman's Wharf, along with a treasury of Californian seafood including lobster, prawns, shrimps, clams and abalone.

Sourdough bread is a white, crusty loaf with a tangy flavour that was a staple food in the Gold Rush days. Unlike the yeast-based baking of today, it uses a starter culture that the miners would take with them on their travels – the term "sourdough" was once used to describe anyone who had spent a winter in Alaska, a legacy of the 1890s Klondike Gold Rush.

DRINKS

Whether you want a cappuccino, a micro-brewed beer, or a Perrier with a twist, the restaurants and cafés of San Francisco can quench your thirst in style

Beer

The locally made brew is Anchor Steam Beer. Specialist bars and restaurants also sell beer made by micro-breweries like Gordon Biersch and the San Francisco Brewing Company (see below). Other Californian beers of distinction are Sierra Nevada Ale and Red Tail Ale.

Wine

When in California drink Californian wine (see page 168). The mark up on bottles served in restaurants is high, so imbibing is best seen as a delicious and necessary learning curve. Waiters are expected to be knowledgeable about the wines they serve, so quiz them relentlessly. Wines are listed by grape variety rather than region – those from the Hess, Landmark and Stag's Leap wineries are a good starting point.

Non-alcoholic drinks

Prepare for a complex choice of fruit juices, fizzy drinks, an endless variety of bottled water, herbal and fruit teas and a splendidly epicurean coffee scene (see page 162).

Water

Tap water is safe to drink but many health-conscious San Franciscans prefer bottled mineral water. Calistoga, from the Napa Valley, is a popular local brand.

BARS

Bars are open at various times between early morning and 2am depending on their location and clientele. The choice runs from sports bars and serious drinkers' dives to yuppie wine bars and rooftop nightclubs. A cocktail on the top floor of an elegant hotel, with the lights of the city and Bay spread below like a blanket of jewels, is a very San Franciscan pleasure. Many bars have a Happy Hour, usually 5pm–7pm.

Carnelian Room

On the 52nd floor of the Bank of America World Headquarters.
555 California Street. Tel: 415/433–7700.

Gordon Biersch

Trendy micro-brewery serving German-style beers made on the premises.
2 Harrison Street. Tel: 415/243–8246.

Hurricane Bar

Grass-roofed huts, mock thunderstorms and live music in the Tonga Room of the Fairmont Hotel.
950 Mason Street. Tel: 415/772–5278.

Pied Piper Bar
Maxfield Parrish's 1909 painting of *The Pied Pier* ignites this clubby bar at the Sheraton Palace Hotel.
2 New Montgomery Street.
Tel: 415/392–8600.

Redwood Room
Art deco redwood paneling, Klimt prints and piano music at the Clift Hotel.
495 Geary Street. Tel: 415/775–4700.

San Francisco Brewing Company
Wood floors, real ale and pub atmosphere.
155 Columbus Avenue. Tel: 415/434–3344.

Top of the Mark
Legendary 19th-floor cocktail bar atop the Mark Hopkins Inter-Continental Hotel on Nob Hill.
California and Mason Streets.
Tel: 415/392–3434.

Vesuvio
An original Beat Generation boozer.
255 Columbus Avenue. Tel: 415/362–3370.

CAFÉS
Bean Scene Café
Mellow sanctuary near Union Square.
582 Sutter Street.
Tel: 415/433–5525.

Blue Monkey Café
Modern coffeehouse with "open mike" evenings.
1777 Steiner Street.
Tel: 415/929–7117.

Brain Wash
Combined launderette and café in SoMa.
1122 Folsom Street.
Tel: 415/861–3663.

Café de la Presse
Lively café selling foreign newspapers and magazines, close to Chinatown Gateway.
352 Grant Avenue. Tel: 415/398–2680.

Caffè Trinity
Coffee and complex Italian sandwiches near the Civic Center.
1 Trinity Center, 1145 Market Street.
Tel: 415/864–3333.

Caffè Trieste
Traditional North Beach haunt for literary bohemians.
609 Vallejo Street. Tel: 415/392–6739.

Jammin' Java
Quintessentially laid-back coffeehouse in the Haight.
701 Cole Street. Tel: 415/668–5282.

Mario's Bohemian Cigar Store Café
Watch Washington Square go by over a cappuccino.
566 Columbus Avenue. Tel: 415/362–0536.

Twin Peaks bar in the Castro

CAFÉ SOCIETY

If at times San Francisco feels like Europe reincarnated, even improved, it is probably due to the presence of so many cafés. The San Franciscans have taken up coffeehouse culture with an enthusiasm verging on the fanatical. There are at least 40 ways to order a coffee here, and, according to the coffee-drinker's bible, *Café San Francisco* by James M Forbes (sold in many cafés), over 250 coffee-drinking venues worth your attention.

The subtitle of this essential caféholic's guide, *How to Learn to Stop Worrying and Live with Little Money*, explains the success of San Franciscan café society. Bohemia may be long dead in Paris and Vienna, but here it is alive and unwell. Like T S Eliot's *Prufrock*, San Franciscans like to measure out their lives with coffee spoons, treating cafés as unofficial community centers where you can find friends, listen to poetry, read the alternative press and

indulge in what is widely considered to be the last vice left in California – caffeine.

So, what'll you have? Why not start with one of the favorite four: Espresso – a neat shot of the black stuff. Cappuccino, an espresso with frothy milk.

Newspapers and poetry readings are an essential part of café culture

Latte, steamed milk with an espresso added. Mocha, a latte with chocolate and cream. But that's just the beginning.

San Francisco's cafés offer everything from street-watching to mystical experiences

Now let's get discerning. How about a twist of lemon on the side of that espresso? Do you want whole or soy milk in that latte? Perhaps you want a touch of vanilla in with the beans? Or maybe you're up for a macchiato (an espresso with a dew-drop of milk), or an iced latte, or some café bianco ... Confused? Have a cup of tea. Now was that regular or herbal ...?

Restaurants

Choosing a restaurant

The San Francisco restaurant scene is a success-hungry world of trailblazing chefs, cutting edge designers and venues that rise and fall like hit records. Dining at the latest hot-spot in the midst of a buzzing in-crowd is a very San Franciscan excitement, but don't be dismayed to find it's booked solid for months. There are an estimated 2,499 other restaurants in the city, and many of them are worth your money.

Chinatown and North Beach are rewarding areas to explore if you like a menu-browsing wander. It is a good idea to make a note of restaurants you meet on your travels – many produce photocopied menus you can take away for perusal. Don't be put off by the idea of dining in the better hotels. Many employ name chefs that have worked their way through a fiercely competitive world, and the service is usually faultless.

The listing below suggests something of the variety available. Local papers and the San Francisco Convention and Visitors Bureau's *San Francisco Book* also have restaurant reviews. Word-of-mouth is especially relevant in a city where many people eat out several times a week, and its compact nature makes it worth traveling a little to get the best. Isolate your target, make a reservation, then run the bath. The symbols below are an indication of restaurant prices. The $ sign represents the approximate cost of a three-course dinner per person with tax but not alcohol or tip. Lunchtime prices are often less.

Cha Cha Cha's in the Haight, where exotic dishes are matched by exotic interiors

$ under 20 dollars
$$ under 30 dollars
$$$ over 30 dollars

Tax of 8.5 percent is added to bills. Tips are not usually included and should be around 15 percent. Always take a taxi home at night.

Abiquiu $$

A valuable oasis in the maelstrom of Downtown; clean-cut décor and tasty New Mexico-inspired cooking.
129 Ellis Street. Tel: 415/392–5500.

Aqua $$$

First class fish and seafood in a trendy ambience. Financial District.
252 California Street. Tel: 415/956–9662. Closed: Saturday lunchtime, Sunday.

Appam $

Delicious Indian home cooking in an easy-going atmosphere. SoMa.
1261 Folsom Street. Tel: 415/626–2798.

Backstage $$

Simple and exquisite Californian dishes with a neat, arty décor to match. Civic Center.
687 McAllister Street. Tel: 415/673–9353. Closed: Saturday lunchtime, Sunday.

Bix $$$

Art deco interiors, live jazz and traditional American fare make a winning recipe. Jackson Square.
56 Gold Street. Tel: 415/433–6300. Closed: Saturday and Sunday lunchtime.

Boulevard $$$

One of the most successful new restaurants in the city with a far-ranging menu and willfully Continental décor. Embarcadero.
1 Mission Street at Steuart Street. Tel: 415/543–6084. Closed: Saturday and Sunday lunchtime.

Brandy Ho's $

Spicy Chinese cooking from Hunan province. North Beach.
450–452 Broadway. Tel: 415/362–6268.

Café Marimba $

Mexican spice and exuberance in the Marina District.
2317 Chestnut Street. Tel: 415/776–1506.

Calzone's $$

Pizzas, classic Italian dishes and picture window views of Columbus Avenue. North Beach.
430 Columbus Avenue. Tel: 415/397–3600.

Cha Cha Cha $$

Cooking with a Caribbean-Cajun twist and exotic shrines on the walls. Haight-Ashbury.
1801 Haight Street. Tel: 415/386–5758.

Charley Brown's $$

Family restaurant in The Cannery, overlooking Fisherman's Wharf.
2801 Leavenworth Street. Tel: 415/776–3838.

City View $

Chinese cooking in a spacious, spotless atmosphere. Chinatown.
662 Commercial Street. Tel: 415/398–2838.

Crown Room $$

On the 24th floor of the Fairmont Hotel, buffet with superb city views.
950 Mason Street. Tel: 415/772–5131.

film *Vertigo*. Financial District.
847 Montgomery Street. Tel: 415/397–5969. Closed: lunchtime and Sunday.

Fly Trap $$
Bentwood chairs, white tablecloths, traditional San Franciscan dishes, satisfied grins. SoMa.
606 Folsom Street. Tel: 415/243–0580. Closed: Saturday lunchtime, Sunday.

Fog City Diner $$
Californian cuisine in a restaurant resembling a chrome-faced railroad dining car. Embarcadero.
1300 Battery Street. Tel: 415/982–2000.

Fournou's Ovens $$$
Gourmet American cuisine in the snug comforts of the Stouffer Stanford Court Hotel. Nob Hill.
905 California Street. Tel: 415/989–1910.

Gordon Biersch $$
Tasty California dining in a warehouse turned micro-brewery. Embarcadero.
2 Harrison Street. Tel: 415/243–8246.

Greens $$
First class vegetarian cuisine combined with stunning Bay views. Fort Mason Center.
Building A. Marina Boulevard at Buchanan Street. Tel: 415/771–6222. Closed: Sunday evening, Monday.

Il Fornaio $$
Constantly popular restaurant and speciality bread shop offering definitive Italian fare. North Embarcadero.
1265 Battery Street. Tel: 415/986–0100.

Cypress Club $$$
Classy Californian food in a rich, zany setting inspired by 1940s cartoons.
500 Jackson Street. Tel: 415/296–8555. Closed: lunchtime.

Elka $$$
Memorable East-meets-West fish and seafood served in the calm of the Miyako Hotel. Japantown.
1611 Post Street. Tel: 415/922–7788.

Equinox $$
Revolving restaurant on the roof of the Hyatt Regency Hotel, serving food for all tastes including Sunday brunch.
5 Embarcadero Center. Tel: 415/788–1234.

Ernie's $$$
Contemporary French cuisine in a refined location used in Hitchcock's

John's Grill $$
Cozy, photo-lined chophouse, mentioned in Dashiell Hammett's *The Maltese Falcon*. Downtown.
63 Ellis Street. Tel: 415/986–0069. Closed: Sunday lunchtime.

LuLu $$
Thought-about Californian cuisine in a buzzing, in-crowd atmosphere. SoMa.
816 Folsom Street. Tel: 415/495–5775. Closed: Sunday lunchtime.

McCormick and Kuleto's $$
Superlative choice of fish and seafood complemented by splendid views of the Bay. Ghirardelli Square.
900 North Point Street. Tel: 415/929–1730.

Millennium $$
Pioneering vegan cuisine and organic wine served in the modish basement of the Abigail Hotel. Civic Center.
246 McAllister Street. Tel: 415/487–9800. Closed: Monday night.

Mooses $$$
Contemporary Italian cuisine and a big, happy atmosphere. Washington Square.
1652 Stockton Street. Tel: 415/989–7800.

Pane e Vino $$
Stylish Italian trattoria in Union Street, good for pasta or fish moods. ⸜
3011 Steiner Street. Tel: 415/346–2111. Closed: Sunday lunchtime.

Rumpus $$
Good value, nonsense-free dishes in a friendly, bistro-style ambience. Downtown.
1 Tillman Place (off Grant Avenue). Tel: 415/421–2300.

Silks $$$
Heavenly Californian-Asian cuisine at the Mandarin Oriental Hotel – the best gourmet dining in town. Financial District.
222 Sansome Street. Tel: 415/986–2020. Closed: Saturday lunchtime.

Stinking Rose $$
Paradise for garlic-lovers, where "it's chic to reek." North Beach.
325 Columbus Avenue. Tel: 415/781–7673.

Tadich Grill $$
San Franciscan institution serving dependable fish and seafood in a world of shiny wood and white linen.
240 California Street. Tel: 415/391–1849. Closed: Sunday.

Tommy Toys $$$
Quality Chinese cuisine with French overtones, served in stately rooms evoking Imperial China. By Transamerica Pyramid.
655 Montgomery Street. Tel: 415/397–4888. Closed: Saturday and Sunday lunchtime.

Victor's $$$
Fine dining on the 32nd floor of the Westin St Francis Hotel.
Union Square. Tel: 415/956–7777.

Yank Sing $
Perfect for *dim sum* adventures – reservations essential. Financial District.
427 Battery Street. Tel: 415/781–1111. Closed: evenings.

Zuni Café $$
Ideal for hunger pangs if visiting the Hayes Valley or Civic Center.
1658 Market Street. Tel: 415/552–2522. Closed: Monday.

CALIFORNIA'S WINE

The Spanish missionaries introduced grapevines to California, but winemaking only became a major enterprise after the Gold Rush. The Buena Vista winery in Sonoma, founded in 1857 by a Hungarian count, claims to be the oldest commercial vineyard in the region. Today 90 percent of American wine comes from California, with the best produced in some 270 flagship wineries lining the Napa and Sonoma valleys.

California's viticulture is a tale of European arts tuned to a New World. Settlers from France, Italy, Germany and Eastern Europe imported vine stocks and expertise from their native lands, adapting varieties to suit local soils and fog-bound micro-climates. The greatest part of the Napa and Sonoma vineyards is today given over to producing white Chardonnays and red Cabernet Sauvignons. Zinfandel, a red grape unique to California, is grown extensively in Sonoma.

As winemakers seek new challenges, there is increased diversity – white wines like Chenin Blanc, Sauvignon Blanc and Riesling, and reds such as Merlot and Pinot Noir, are now common varieties. Sparkling wine producers such as Mumm, Freixenet and Moët & Chandon have also started successful ventures here.

The international success of California's wine dates from the 1970s, but despite a phenomenal demand from European markets, Californians still have to work hard to educate their compatriots in the pleasures of imbibing. Wines are promoted by grape type rather than place of origin, and there is a healthy rivalry between dynastic wine families and new "wine brats." While the former are keen to preserve the measured and conservative disciplines of the old school, the latter go in for funky labels, pop industry-style publicity and crusades against wine snobbery. "We make wines that WE like to drink" raps one iconoclastic winery. "Then we set out to find people that like what we like."

In California wine labels have become works of art reflecting the philosophy of each winery

KENWOOD
ARTIST SERIES

KENWOOD
Sonoma Valley
CABERNET SAUVIGNON

GUNDLACH BUNDSCHU
1990
RHINEFARM VINEYARDS
CABERNET SAUVIGNON
SONOMA VALLEY
PRODUCED & BOTTLED BY
GUNDLACH BUNDSCHU WINERY B.W. 64
VINEBURG, CA 95487
ALC 13% BY VOL · CONTAINS SULFITES

KENWOOD
1976 SONOMA COUNTY CABERNET SAUVIGNON
PRODUCED AND BOTTLED BY
KENWOOD VINEYARDS, KENWOOD, CA
Artist Series   Alc. 13.5% by Vol.

Accommodations

*S*an Francisco has been putting visitors up for the night since the Gold Rush, and has a spectacular choice of hotels and other accommodations to please all tastes and budgets.

San Francisco has accommodations to suit all budgets; most hotels are in the Downtown area

WHERE TO STAY

San Francisco is a city of hills, vistas and large, skyscraping hotels. If you don't mind heights and high speed lifts that transplant your stomach to your mouth, there is no better place to stay than on the zillionth floor of a historic hotel with picture window views out to the Bay and its famous bridges.

Most visitors stay in Downtown, on Nob Hill and at Fisherman's Wharf, which are all close to the main sights. Anywhere else will be more relaxed, but may require some traveling in order to reach points of interest. The San Francisco Convention and Visitors Bureau produces an annual *Lodging Guide* that includes comprehensive details about all types of accommodations available in the city and Bay Area.

PRICES

All prices for lodgings in San Francisco are subject to a "transient occupancy" tax of 12 percent. Hotel prices are per room at a single or double rate. Always ask about discount rates in large chain hotels as they never stop having special offers and tariff fluctuations. Expect to pay around $100 for a good-size, quality room. There is no grading system of hotels by stars as in Europe.

Bills are normally settled by credit card – an imprint will be taken on check in. Many hotels now have complete No Smoking floors. Breakfast is rarely included in the price of a room. Telephone and parking charges vary considerably from hotel to hotel.

CHILDREN

In many cases children sharing with their parents are included in the room price, but age limits vary from hotel to hotel. Many hotels provide babysitting services and special children's programs.

RESERVATIONS

San Francisco is a busy city, so don't be surprised if your favorite hotel is completely filled by some bigwig's retinue or a convention of pneumatic drill manufacturers.

Reservations are normally made by telephoning direct and leaving your credit card number. Hotels will usually hold a room reservation until 6pm – if you plan to arrive later it is customary to let them know. Chain hotels and

The San Remo Hotel in North Beach is a restored 1906 Victorian building furnished with antiques

discount agencies have their own central reservations numbers, many of which are toll-free.

Best Western
Tel: 1–800/528–1234.

Central Reservation Service
Tel: 1–800/548–3311; 407/339–4116.

Discount Hotel Rates
Tel: 1–800/576–0003.

Holiday Inn
Tel: 1–800/465–4329.

Hyatt Hotels
Tel: 1–800/233–1234.

ITT Sheraton
Tel: 1–800/325–3535.

Ramada Hotels
Tel: 1–800/228–8408.

Travelodge
Tel: 1–800/578–7878.

THE HIGH LIFE

Riding the elevators in San Francisco's skyscraping grand hotels can be as thrilling as a funfair ride. Some slide up and down the outside of the building, with glass windows providing sudden and sensational views. The five that rocket up to the 32nd floor of the Tower Building at the Westin St Francis Hotel in Union Square travel at a rate of 1,000 feet a minute, and there is similar free fun at The Fairmont Hotel on Nob Hill, where the glass elevator at its east end shoots up 24 storys. Interior elevators can also be exciting, notably those within the staggering atrium of the Hyatt Regency Hotel in the Embarcadero Center.

Grand Hotels

Many of San Francisco's best-known landmarks are grand hotels, worth visiting for a whiff of history, luxury and ongoing success. You don't need to be a guest to enter – they all have quality restaurants, or just drop by for afternoon tea, a cocktail in the bar or Sunday brunch.

The city's grandest hotel no longer exists. The legendary 800-room, seven-story Palace Hotel opened in Market Street in 1875, but burnt down in the aftermath of the 1906 earthquake. Its site is now filled by the imperious **Sheraton Palace**, opened in 1909, where the stained glass-covered Garden Court restaurant recalls its dignified predecessor.

The **Westin St Francis** in Union Square is an equally venerable hotel, founded in 1904 by the millionaire Crocker family. The ancient Austrian clock in its lobby is a well-known San Franciscan point of rendezvous. Close by in Geary Street, the **Clift** is another historic luxury hotel; opened in 1915, its 1934 wood-panelled Redwood Room is an art deco masterpiece.

Many more grand hotels gather around Nob Hill. The **Fairmont** in Mason Street opened in 1907, and in nearby Stockton Street the **Ritz-Carlton** boasts the majestic neo-classical 1909 façade of the former Metropolitan Life building. The **Stouffer-Stanford Court** in California Street occupies a 1912 apartment building, while the purpose-built **Mark Hopkins Inter-Continental**, alias "The

The Mark Hopkins Inter-Continental Hotel

Ancient and modern grandeur: the Garden Court at the Sheraton Palace (left); lobby at the Mandarin (below)

Regency in the Embarcadero Center featuring a spectacular lobby. He also designed the 21-story **Pan-Pacific** (1987) in Post Street. The **Marriot** in Market Street opened in 1989 and was swiftly christened "The Jukebox" by locals. In the Financial District, the **Mandarin Oriental**'s rooms fill the top 11 floors of the fog-piercing 48-story First Interstate Center, and are as near to heaven as it's safe to go.

Mark," dates from 1926 and occupies the peak of Nob Hill. Its rooftop cocktail bar, designed by Timothy Pfleuger 13 years later, is a legendary venue for skyscraper partying.

More recent additions to this illustrious lineage include John Portman's innovative 1973 **Hyatt**

HOTELS
Art hotels
Small, speciality hotels appealing to an arts, music and media-conscious clientele are a growing feature of the San Francisco hotel scene. Downtown examples include the Hotel Triton, kitted out with zany furniture and contemporary art, the Diva, which includes a condom in its welcoming gifts, and the slickly Italian Hotel Milano in SoMa. The Phoenix Inn in the Tenderloin is a converted no-tell motel favored by top rock stars.

Boutique hotels
Distancing themselves from the monster chain hotels catering to business customers and tour groups, boutique hotels are small, individual affairs that usually occupy a historic building and

Rooms at the Red Victorian Bed and Breakfast in the Haight are decorated in Sixties style

The Red Victorian
Bed & Breakfast

San Francisco

often come furnished with English country house comforts. Some like to call themselves "Inns" to emphasize their logs-on-the-fire individuality. Examples are the waterfront Harbor Court Hotel, the Tuscan Inn near Fisherman's Wharf and the Kensington Park Hotel near Union Square.

Business hotels
See page 177.

Grand hotels
See pages 172–3.

Motels
Designed as economical pit-stops where the passing motorist can get some shut-eye, motels are now being rediscovered as inoffensive bases for a budget vacation. Many of them are lined up along Lombard Street and include free parking in their rates.

Neighborhood hotels
You don't have to stay in the whirlpool of the city center. Every San Francisco neighborhood has its small local hotels where things are more relaxed and you can get a feel of the community. Examples include the hippy chic Red Victorian Inn in Haight-Ashbury, the Beat Generation Bohème in North Beach, the Miyako in Japantown and the quietly pampering Nob Hill Lambourne.

BED AND BREAKFAST
B&B's are a popular choice with tourists visiting San Francisco. They offer an elegant, unique alternative to hotels. Some San Francisco "Bed and Breakfast Inns" offer extremely lavish accommodation, and are often in restored Victorians with antique furnishings and a wealthy mansion feel.

The Bay Area has plenty of motels where you can spend an inexpensive night

Examples are the Alamo Square Inn, and in Pacific Heights, the Bed and Breakfast Inn and Art Center Bed and Breakfast.

Bed and Breakfast International
PO Box 282910, San Francisco CA 94128–2910. Tel: 1–800/872–4500; 415/696–1690.

APARTMENTS
If you want an apartment for a short-term vacation or business rental, there are specialist agencies you can contact. You can also stay in suite-only hotels where rooms have kitchen facilities, such as the Hyde Park Suites near Aquatic Park in Hyde Street, or Brady Acres in Downtown. Renting an apartment in San Francisco for a long stay is best done once you're here – look in the newspaper advertisements and ask around. Prices for a room in shared accommodation are reasonable.

American Property Exchange
170 Page Street. Tel: 415/863–8484.

HOSTELS
Hostels offer accommodation for all travelers, though their budget prices and communal facilities mean they are most popular with students and the young. Those belonging to the American Youth Hostel organization (AYH) are part of the worldwide youth hosteling network. Guests usually take their own sleeping bag.

Golden Gate AYH Hostel
Marin Headlands
Fort Barry, Building 941. Tel: 415/331–2777.

San Francisco International AYH Hostel
Dormitory accommodation in Civil War-era army barracks.
Fort Mason, Building 240. Tel: 415/771–7277.

CAMPING
There are no campsites in San Francisco city but recreational camping is available in State Parks such as Angel Island, Mount Tamalpais and at Half Moon Bay. For general information contact the California Department of Parks and Recreation, tel: 916/653–6995. For reservations call MISTIX, tel: 1–800/444–7275.

On Business

A major commercial, financial and tourist center, San Francisco is a progressive city where business and leisure are easily combined. It is regularly used for conventions by companies and institutions.

BANKS
Normally open Monday to Friday 10am–3pm, with some offering extended hours and a Saturday morning service. Money can also be changed in travel agencies and hotels. Take your passport or some form of identification.

Thomas Cook Currency Services
75 Geary Street. Tel: 415/362–3452.
Pier 39, Jefferson Street. Tel:
415/362–6271.

BUSINESS HOURS
Normally Monday to Friday 9am–5pm, but many business people start work earlier.

BUSINESS SERVICES
Ideas Unlimited (concierge services). Tel: 415/668–7089.
Lingualink Inc (interpreting), 388 Market Street, Suite 400. Tel: 415/431–9222.
Mail Boxes Etc (packaging and shipping), 268 Bush Street. Tel: 415/765–1515.
President Tuxedo (formal wear), 170 Sutter Street. Tel: 415/989–7642.
Somewhere in Time (florists), 699 Folsom Street. Tel: 415/882–9696.

COURIER SERVICES
Federal Express (air courier), 677 Howard Street. Tel: 1–800/238–5355.
Special T Delivery (messenger service), PO Box 422127. Tel: 415/861–2225.

CONFERENCE AND EXHIBITION FACILITIES
Cow Palace
Multi-purpose venue at the southern city limits used for trade shows, music, sports, and entertainment.

Geneva Avenue and Santos Street. Tel: 415/469–6065.

Moscone Convention Center
Part of the Yerba Buena Gardens complex (see page 91).
744 Howard Street. Tel: 415/974–4000.

DRESS
Look good but don't get hung up about it – a sartorial philosophy borne out by the many businesswomen who arrive every morning by commuter ferry sporting power suits and gym shoes, the latter being swapped for chic heels left in the office drawer. Suits and ties are the norm in the Financial District and business-orientated restaurants.

ETIQUETTE
Californians express their enthusiasm and positive feelings without fear, and may misinterpret traditional Eastern reserve as a negative reaction. They often arrive early for appointments – and if they arrive on time, you can bet they'll apologize for being late.

Lunch is a central part of business life, and a prime reason for San Francisco's gastronomic vitality. If you are the host don't be afraid to ask your guests to suggest a few possible restaurants they might like to try. Business colleagues may well invite you to their homes or to social activities in the evening or on weekends – it's all part of the West Coast good life where work and play never cease.

HOTELS
With so many San Francisco hotels competing for business travelers, there are always new services and incentives

You've made it when they send a stretch limo

Pacific Stock Exchange

to entice you here rather than there – perhaps a complimentary morning limousine to the Financial District, access to club class floors, free family accommodation. If you have the time, it will pay to shop around.

All large hotels will have a conference room and currency exchange, and be able to book car rental, restaurants and excursions. Hotels and their restaurants are often used as venues for meetings, and many have business floors, satellite TV, business centers and audiovisual equipment. More and more are offering in-room fax, modem and computer links.

Almost every hotel accepts credit cards, but advance reservations are essential, especially at smaller Bed and Breakfast establishments. Check-in time for guests in most hotels tends to be around 3pm.

TRAVEL ARRANGEMENTS
American Express Travel Agency, 237 Post Street. Tel: 415/981–5533.
Columbus Travel, 507 Columbus Avenue. Tel: 415/398–2322.

Practical Guide

FOR VISITORS
FROM OVERESEAS

ARRIVING
Documents

All travelers must be in possession of a valid passport. British citizens arriving by air are granted a visa waiver, but will need one if arriving in the US by other means. Citizens of Australia and South Africa also require visas, which should be obtained in your country of residence.

Visas are free and last the life of your passport. American immigration laws are strict and if you have any questions consult your nearest US Consulate before departure. See also **Health and Insurance**, page 182.

By air

San Francisco International Airport is 14 miles south of the city center in San Bruno, and receives flights from many cities around the world and within the US. There are also international airports at Oakland and San Jose.

Airport facilities

San Francisco airport is divided into three linked terminals: North, International and South. Departures are from the upper level and Arrivals on the lower. The airport has a full range of facilities including shops, car rental, hotel booking services and tourist information booths in the Arrivals halls.
Airport Information, tel: 415/761–0800.
Parking Information, tel: 415/761–0270.
Thomas Cook Foreign Exchange, tel: 415/583–4029. Virgin Atlantic Information, tel: 1–800/862–8621.

Airport transfers

The SFO Airporter bus departs from the lower level by stops marked in blue and serves major Downtown hotels. Private shuttle buses depart from both upper and lower levels and take passengers to wherever they are staying. Shuttle buses can be called to pick you up when you depart.
SFO Airporter, tel: 415/495–8404.
Door to Door Airport Express, tel: 415/775–5121.

Virgin Atlantic is one of several major international airlines serving San Francisco

Quake City Shuttle, tel: 415/255–4899.
Super Shuttle, tel: 415/558–8500.

By coach
The legendary Greyhound Bus runs services between San Francisco and numerous destinations. The cheap, slow and alternative Green Tortoise travels similar routes. For other Bay Area services see **Public Transportation**, page 188. Coaches depart from the Transbay Terminal at 425 Mission Street.
Greyhound Lines, tel: 415/558–6789 or 1–800/231–2222. Green Tortoise, tel: 415/821–0833 or 1–800/227–4766.

By rail
Amtrak rail services connect San Francisco with Los Angeles, Seattle and Chicago. A bus service from the Transbay Terminal connects at Oakland with the main coast line. There is a ticket office at the Transbay Terminal, 425 Mission Street.
Amtrak Information, tel: (toll-free) 1–800/872–7245.

The city's railway station is at Fourth and Townsend Streets, and is the terminus for services operated by CalTrain to San Jose (see page 188).

The bi-monthly *Thomas Cook Overseas Timetable* gives details of many rail, bus and shipping services worldwide and can help you plan rail travel in the USA. It is available from any Thomas Cook branch in the UK, and in the US from the Forsyth Travel Library, PO Box 2975, 9154 West 57th Street, Kansas 66201. Tel: 1–800/367–7982.

By road
From the south, Highway 1 is the most scenic route from Los Angeles, with the parallel US 101 a faster inland alternative. From the north, US 101 runs south from Eureka to cross the Golden Gate Bridge, and Interstate 80 runs southwest from Sacramento over the Bay Bridge.

By sea
San Francisco is frequently included in the itineraries of cruise ships – a good travel agent can supply up-to-date details. Ships normally dock at Pier 35.

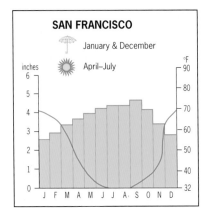

SAN FRANCISCO

January & December

April–July

inches
6
5
4
3
2
1
0
J F M A M J J A S O N D

°F
90
80
70
60
50
40
32

WEATHER CONVERSION CHART
25.4mm = 1 inch
°F = 1.8 × °C + 32

CLIMATE

San Francisco is a year-round vacation destination, but its summer fog creates an idiosyncratic climate that can produce many weathers in a single day. Winters are often wet, summers always markedly cooler than the rest of California. Temperatures rarely fall below 5°C (40°F) or rise above 21°C (70°F).
Weather Information – tel: 415/936–1212.

CONSULATES

Australia
1 Bush Street, 7th Floor. Tel: 415/362–6160.
Germany
1960 Jackson Street. Tel: 415/775–1061.
Ireland
655 Montgomery Street, Suite 930. Tel: 415/392–4214.
UK
1 Sansome Street, Suite 850. Tel: 415/981–3030.

CONVERSION TABLES

Imperial measurements are used in America. The only difference from their UK equivalents is that gallon, quart and pint measures are 20 percent less.

CRIME

Like many cities, San Francisco has its crime problem. Common-sense precautions can help ensure a trouble-free visit, such as always using hotel safe deposit boxes, never carrying more money than necessary (use credit cards and refundable traveler's checks rather than cash), and avoiding confrontational situations on the street.

The risk of crime is greatest at night: never walk alone down dark or deserted streets. Areas to avoid in particular are the Tenderloin, Western Addition, Potrero, Mission and SoMa. If you are going to a restaurant or venue in these areas, take a cab both ways. Don't hang around on the street expecting one to pass – get someone to a call a cab company when you want to leave. If you rent a car, leave no valuables inside and never give rides to hitch-hikers.

CUSTOMS REGULATIONS

The most common customs regulation met by visitors to the United States is the ban on importing fresh fruit. All visitors are required to fill in a customs declaration form on arrival, and it is illegal to import meat, meat products, plants and seeds. Some medication available over the counter abroad, which is prescription-only in the US, may be confiscated by US customs officials unless you have a doctor's note.

Duty-free allowances for travelers over 21 entering the country are 1 liter of spirits, 200 cigarettes or 50 cigars (not Cuban) and $100-worth of gifts.

Men's Suits

UK		36	38	40	42	44	46 48
Rest of Europe	46	48	50	52	54	56	58
US		36	38	40	42	44	46 48

Dress Sizes

UK		8	10	12	14	16	18
France			36	38	40	42	44 46
Italy			38	40	42	44	46 48
Rest of Europe			34	36	38	40	42 44
US		6	8	10	12	14	16

Men's Shirts

UK	14	14.5	15	15.5	16	16.5	17
Rest of Europe	36	37	38	39/40	41	42	43
US	14	14.5	15	15.5	16	16.5	17

Men's Shoes

UK		7	7.5	8.5	9.5	10.5	11
Rest of Europe	41	42	43	44		45	46
US		8	8.5	9.5	10.5	11.5	12

Women's Shoes

UK	4.5	5	5.5	6	6.5	7
Rest of Europe	38	38	39	39	40	41
US	6	6.5	7	7.5	8	8.5

Conversion Table

FROM	TO	MULTIPLY BY
Inches	Centimeters	2.54
Feet	Meters	0.3048
Yards	Meters	0.9144
Miles	Kilometers	1.6090
Acres	Hectares	0.4047
Gallons (US)	Liters	3.7854
Ounces	Grams	28.35
Pounds	Grams	453.6
Pounds	Kilograms	0.4536
Tons	Tonnes	1.0160

To convert back, for example from centimeters to inches, divide by the number in the third column.

DRESS

Take clothes for spring-like weather, and bear in mind that it can be cold on the ferries, Golden Gate Bridge and when the fogs of summer roll in. Most Californians like to dress smart but casual – some top restaurants expect men to wear a jacket and tie.

DRIVING

Car rental

If you are visiting on a package vacation, try to arrange car rental before you leave home, but be aware that seemingly unavoidable add-on charges can virtually double your original bill. Check the figures before you pay, and demand explanations if necessary. All bills are subject to 8.5 percent sales tax.

Drivers must hold a valid driver's licence and be over 21. You will also need a credit card to provide a deposit, though some companies may accept a substantial cash amount instead. All rental cars have automatic gears – if you are unfamiliar with these ask for a few minutes instruction before hitting the road. Gas in the US is cheap by European standards, and virtually all rental cars take unleaded. Gas stations are not as common as you might expect, so fill up before you set off for, say, Point Reyes National Seashore.

Alamo, 687 Folsom Street. Tel: 415/882–9440.
Associated Limousines, 1398 Bryant Street. Tel: 415/563–1000.
Budget Rent-a-Car, 321 Mason Street. Tel: 415/775–5800.
Dollar, 364 O'Farrell Street. Tel: 415/771–5300.
Dubbelju (motorcycles), 271 Clara Street. Tel: 415/495–2774.
Hertz, 433 Mason Street. Tel: 415/771–2200.

On the road

Drive on the right. The maximum speed limit is 55 miles per hour (88 kph). Seat belts are compulsory in front seats. San Francisco's grid of streets includes steep hills and a convoluted one-way system – remember that cable cars have right of way. There is a toll for drivers coming south across the Golden Gate Bridge. *California Road Conditions, tel: 415/557–3755.*

Parking

Parking restrictions are enforced with vigor. Look up to check signs detailing street-cleaning times and tow-away zones, then down for the color of the curb. Anywhere painted red, yellow, yellow-and-black, yellow-and-black-and-green, blue (unless you are a disabled driver), white and green (unless you are stopping five or 10 minutes respectively) are out. If you find anything in between all this, grab it!

San Francisco has many off-street and multi-story parking garages who advertize their prices with loud signs, or you can chance your luck finding a meter in the street. "Valet Parking," where hotels and restaurants charge to park your car for you, is common, and many shopping centres offer "Validated Parking," where parking is free or discounted if you show a purchase receipt on departure.

When parking on the city's steep hills, you are required by law to turn your vehicle's front wheels into the curb facing downhill, to the street facing uphill. Don't forget the handbrake.

ELECTRICITY

Standard electrical supply in the US is 110 volts (60 cycles). Sockets take flat two-pin plugs, so UK and European appliances will need an adaptor.

EMERGENCY TELEPHONE NUMBERS

Dial 911 for Police, Fire and Ambulance services.

The Thomas Cook Worldwide Customer Promise offers free emergency assistance at any Thomas Cook network location to travelers who have purchased their travel tickets at a Thomas Cook Network location. In addition, as a free service under the Thomas Cook Mastercard International Alliance, any Mastercard cardholder may use any Thomas Cook Network location to report the loss or theft of their card and obtain an emergency replacement.

Thomas Cook Mastercard Refund Centre, tel: 1–800/223–7373 (toll free, 24-hour service). Loss or theft should be reported within 24 hours.

HEALTH AND INSURANCE

There are no mandatory vaccination requirements for entering the US, but tetanus and polio immunisation should be kept up to date. Like many parts of the world, AIDS is present. The latest health advice can be obtained from your Thomas Cook travel consultant.
If you need to consult a doctor or dentist ask at your hotel or look in the Yellow Pages telephone directory.

St Francis Memorial Hospital, 900 Hyde Street. Tel: 415/353–6000.

San Francisco General Hospital, 1001 Potrero Avenue. Tel: 415/206–8000.

San Francisco Dental Office, 132 Embarcadero (between Mission and Howard Streets). Tel: 415/777–5115.

Pharmacies

Drugstores are a common feature of San Francisco's streets and sell a multitude of over-the-counter medications. Most have a pharmacist on duty who can dispense prescriptions.

24-hour pharmacies:
Walgreens, 498 Castro Street. Tel: 415/861–3136.
Walgreens, 3201 Divisadero Street. Tel: 415/931–6417.

Insurance
Adequate medical insurance is highly recommended, and a pretravel requirement with many packaged tours. Medical care in the US is very expensive. In the UK travel insurance policies, which include healthcare, can be purchased through the AA, branches of Thomas Cook and most travel agents.

LOST PROPERTY
If you lose anything of value inform the police, if only for insurance purposes. The loss of a passport should be reported to your consulate. For traveler's checks see **Emergency Telephone Numbers**, page 180.
MUNI Lost and Found (public transport), tel: 415/923–6168.

MAPS
Free city maps are available from the San Francisco Visitor Information Center, see page 25. Rand McNally publishes several maps useful for touring the Bay Area, and the *Napa Sonoma Wine Country Touring Map* (H M Gousha) shows the exact location of wineries in the two counties. For bookshops see page 142.

MEDIA
Newspapers and magazines
The city has two daily papers: the morning *San Francisco Chronicle* and the afternoon *San Francisco Examiner*. On

Sundays they combine to produce a wrist-wearying tome that can number 16 parts. Useful supplements include the Wednesday *Food* sections and the pink Sunday *Datebook* which contains the latest what's on listings.

Free weekly papers dispensed from curbside stands at major commuter points provide helpful and absorbing reading. The *Bay Guardian* and *SF Weekly* are bibles of San Francisco's alternative scene and the best source of offbeat poetry readings, live music and nightlife. Numerous monthly magazines, like *SF Focus* and *Bay City*, are pitched at visiting tourists and also contain cultural listings.

Catch up on local news and events with San Francisco's two daily newspapers

TV and radio
Don't stay in to watch American television, which has countless channels but little essential viewing. If you want to relax, many hotels have videos for rent of films starring San Francisco. The choice of radio stations is even more prolific, and you can usually find something to while away the traffic jams or underscore a scenic drive. Start your sampling with some jazz from KJAZ (92.7 FM),

Bank of America has its world headquarters in San Francisco's Financial District

parking meters and other coin-operated machines.

Traveler's checks

Thomas Cook MasterCard traveler's checks avoid the hazards of carrying large amounts of cash, and can be quickly refunded in the event of their loss or theft (see emergency refund number on page 182, and help locations below). Traveler's checks must be denominated in US dollars, and are widely accepted in lieu of cash.

The following branches of Thomas Cook can provide emergency assistance in the case of loss or theft of Thomas Cook MasterCard traveler's checks, as well as providing foreign exchange facilities.

Thomas Cook Foreign Exchange, 75 Geary Street. Tel: 415/362–3452.
Thomas Cook Foreign Exchange, Building M, Level 2, Pier 39, Fisherman's Wharf. Tel: 415/362–6271.

Credit cards

Credit cards are so widely used in America that travel can become difficult if you do not own at least one in a major name. A card imprint or swipe will normally be taken when you rent a car or check into a hotel, and in some cases, such as when you rent a bicycle or drink at an upmarket bar, you will be asked to surrender the card until you settle your bill later.

Taxes

Taxes vary from state to state in the US. In California there is an 8.5 percent sales tax on all purchases except food for preparation. Hotel bills are subject to a

country and western from KSAN (94.5 FM) and rock from KFOG (104.5 FM). News and talk is carried on the AM band by stations like KGO (810 AM).

MONEY MATTERS
Currency

The American unit of currency is the dollar ($), divided into 100 cents (¢) Banknotes are issued for 1 (a buck), 2, 5, 10, 20, 50 and 100 dollars; coins for 1 (a penny), 5 (a nickel), 10 (a dime), 25 (a quarter) and 50 cents. All banknotes are printed the same size and color, so be vigilant. Keep a stock of quarters for

12 percent transient tax. There is no airport or departure tax.

OPENING TIMES

Banks are open at least Monday to Friday 10am–3pm, see page 176. For shops see page 140. The favored closing day for museums is Monday.

PLACES OF WORSHIP

Many religions, both old and new, have churches in San Francisco. Ask at your hotel or the San Francisco Visitor Information Center for locations and service times.

See also entries for Grace Cathedral, St Mary's Cathedral and Old St Mary's Church (Chinatown).

POLICE

Police wear dark blue uniforms, carry arms and are there to help.
Emergency: 911.
Non-emergency: 415/553–0123.

POST OFFICES

Post offices are usually open Monday to Friday 9am–5pm and Saturday 9am–1pm but times vary with location. The most aesthetic venue to carry out transactions is amid the 1940s murals of the Rincon Center (see page 141). Stamps can also be bought from hotels, vending machines and some shops. Mail boxes are dark blue and often have only one collection a day.

Letters for collection (*poste restante*), which should be marked "General Delivery," can be sent to San Francisco General Mail Facility, 3801 Third Street, San Francisco CA 94105-9602. Tel: 415/543–0121.

May the law be with you: San Francisco police officer

PUBLIC HOLIDAYS

January 1 New Year's Day
3rd Monday in January Martin Luther King Jr Day
3rd Monday in February President's Day
March/April Easter Sunday and Monday
Last Monday in May Memorial Day
July 4 Independence Day
1st Monday in September Labor Day
2nd Monday in October Columbus Day
November 11 Veteran's Day
4th Thursday in November Thanksgiving Day
December 25 Christmas Day

PUBLIC TRANSPORTATION

Public transportation in San Francisco is operated by MUNI, who produce free timetables and an inexpensive *Street and Transit Map* listing all routes and connections, available from Metro stations, MUNI kiosks and some bookstores. Discount fares apply if over 65 or under 18. Under-fives travel free. For details of MUNI Passports, and for taxis, see page 23. For ferries see page 132.

MUNI Information, tel: 415/673–6864.

Bus

Bus stops are indicated by an orange MUNI sign or a yellow stripe on lamp-posts. Board at the front and exit at the rear. There is a flat fare of $1 – show your pass, punch your ticket or pay cash as you enter (drivers give no change). If you want to change buses ask the driver for a transfer on your ticket, which allows for two more trips in the time period shown. When you get off, you need to step down to the door to make it open automatically.

Metro

MUNI operates five streetcar routes that combine subway and surface travel, each designated by letters from J to M. Tickets can be bought from machines in Metro stations or on board if above ground.

Cable cars

There are three lines – look carefully at the painted signs on the cars to get the right route. Stops are marked by brown signs with a cable car picture. Tickets cost $2 with no transfers permitted. The crew have designated areas that have to be kept clear, marked by yellow lines on the floor – if you stand in them, expect to hear about it. See pages 26–7.

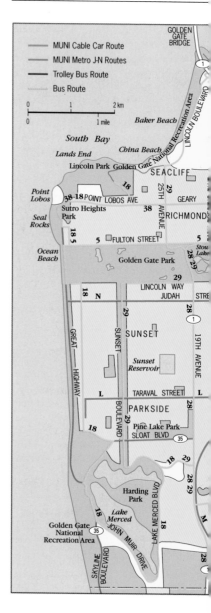

—— MUNI Cable Car Route
—— MUNI Metro J-N Routes
—— Trolley Bus Route
······ Bus Route

MUNI AND BART TRANSPORT

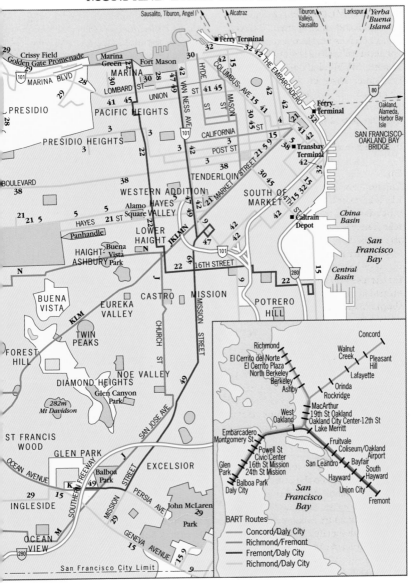

BART

The four lines of the Bay Area Rapid Transit System link 15 cities in three counties around the Bay Area. Tickets are bought from station machines – you can add to their value later. Trains carry the name of their final destination. *BART Information, tel: 415/788–2278.*

Bay Area

If you are traveling extensively in the Bay Area by public transport, get a copy of the inexpensive *San Francisco Bay Area Regional Transit Guide* published by the Metropolitan Transport Commission, available from bookstores.

AC Transit

Bus services to Berkeley, Oakland and the East Bay.
Tel: 1–800/559–4636.

Amador Stage Lines

Bus services to Reno via Oakland.
Tel: 1–800/722–2877.

CalTrain

Rail services between San Francisco and San Jose.
Tel: 1–800/660–4287.

Golden Gate Transit

Bus and ferry services to Marin and Sonoma Counties.
Tel: 415/332–6600.

SamTrans

Bus services in San Mateo County.
Tel: 1–800/660–4287.

Santa Clara Co. Transportation Agency

Bus services in San Jose and Santa Clara County.
Tel: 1–800/894–9908.

TELEPHONES

Local telephone calls are cheap, so treat the phone as a sightseeing tool that can be used for checking opening times and transport arrangements, and for making reservations for shows and restaurants. The rates charged by hotels for calls from your room vary considerably – check the fees before you dial to avoid a shock on departure.

Some numbers are advertised with easy to remember letters replacing the last four digits, such as 415/673–MUNI. Look for the letter on the phone and dial the corresponding number. Those prefixed 1–800 are toll-free. Reverse charge calls, arranged through the operator, are called "collect."

Payphones

Public telephones take 5, 10 and 25 cent coins, and some accept credit cards. Most bars have a payphone too.

Dialing codes

The area code for San Francisco is 415. If you are calling from within the city you do not need to use it. The code for Oakland and the East Bay is 510. To call long distance within the US dial 1 then the area code and number.

To call abroad from the US dial 011, then the country code, then the number omitting any initial 0. Some international codes are: Australia 61, France 33, Germany 49, Irish Republic 353, Mexico 52, New Zealand 64, South Africa 27, UK 44. No code is necessary to call Canada from the US.

Operator: 0
Directory Assistance (local): 411
Directory Assistance (long-distance): dial 1 then area code then 555–1212.

TIME

California is in the Pacific Standard Time zone, which is 8 hours behind GMT. When it is noon in San Francisco it is 3pm in New York and 8pm in London. The clocks are put forward one hour from the last Sunday in April to the first Sunday in October. For the exact time, tel: 767–2676 (POP–CORN).

TIPPING

Tipping is expected in America, but do as you feel the service merits. Suitable amounts are $1 a bag for a porter, 15 percent for taxis and in restaurants.

TOILETS

Public toilets are commonly known as Rest Rooms.

TOURIST INFORMATION

Overseas

For information on San Francisco before you leave home, there are US Tourist Offices in many cities around the world. A few are devoted specifically to California, including:

Germany: MSI, Leibigstrasse 8, 60323 Frankfurt/Main. Tel: 69–72770.
UK: Californian Tourism Information Office, Suite 433, High Holborn House, 52–4 High Holborn, London WC1V 6RB. Tel: 0171–242 2838.

California

California Division of Tourism, PO Box 1499, Sacramento, CA 95812–1499. Tel: 916/322–1397.

San Francisco

See page 25. Postal inquiries should be sent to PO Box 429097, San Francisco, CA 94142–9097. See individual entries for tourist offices in the Bay Area.

TRAVELERS WITH DISABILITIES

San Francisco is one of the most accessible cities in the world for disabled visitors. Most transport services, including airport shuttle buses, MUNI buses and BART stations and trains have facilities for wheelchairs, and many public buildings have purpose-built access. Information on services for the disabled are available by telephone – numbers prefixed TDD are for users with impaired hearing.

Information

Disability Coordinator, Mayor's Office of Community Development.
10 United Nations Plaza, Suite 600, San Francisco CA 94102. Tel: 415/554–8925, TDD tel: 415/554–8749.
MUNI Accessible Service Programs (public transportation).
949 Presidio Avenue, San Francisco CA 94115. Tel: 415/932–6142.
San Francisco Convention & Visitors Bureau.
TTD/TTY tel: 415/392–0328.
Easter Seal Society (information).
Tel: 415/752–4888.

USEFUL TELEPHONE NUMBERS

Airport Information (SFO):
415/761–8000.
Airport Shuttle (Super Shuttle):
415/558–8500.
Amtrak: 1–800/872–7245.
BART: 415/788–2278.
Ferries: see page 132.
San Francisco Convention and Visitors Bureau: 451/391–2000.
Taxi (Yellow Cab): 415/626–2345.
Time: 415/767–8900.
US Customs: 415/705–4440.
Western Union (money transfer):
1–800/325–6000.

ACKNOWLEDGMENTS

The Automobile Association wishes to thank the following photographers, libraries and associations for their assistance in the preparation of this book.

ASSOCIATED PRESS/TOPHAM 55c; **BOCCON-GIBOD** 179; **GORDON BIERSCH BREWERY AND RESTAURANT** 166; **MANDARIN ORIENTAL HOTEL** 173b; **MARY EVANS PICTURE LIBRARY** 12,12/3; **REX FEATURES** 64a, 64b, 65; **SAN FRANCISCO CARTOON ART MUSEUM** 42; **SAN FRANCISCO CHRONICLE** 15; **SAN FRANCISCO CONVENTION AND VISITORS BUREAU (Kerrick James)** 154; **THE KOBAL COLLECTION** 148a, 148b; **THE RONALD GRANT ARCHIVE** 34, 149a, 149b; **TOPHAM PICTUREPOINT** 55d, 64.

All remaining pictures are held in the Association's own library and were taken by **KEN PATERSON** with the exception of pages 6, 16, 35, 39, 44/5, 45d, 113a, 113b, 117, 119, 134/5, 136, 137, 150, 177 which were taken by **ROBERT HOLMES** and 93, 169 which were taken by **NIGEL TISDALL**.

The author would like to thank the following organizations and individuals for their assistance:
Sharon Rooney, Dawn Stranne, Helen Chang and the staff of the San Francisco Convention & Visitors Bureau; the San Jose Convention & Visitors Bureau; Californian Tourism Information Office, London; Virgin Atlantic; Jeffrey Nead; Tessa Souter; Alice Prier; John Browne.

The author and series adviser would like to thank the following hotels for their assistance while researching this book: Westin St Francis; Mandarin Oriental; Ritz-Carlton; Clift; Pan-Pacific; Hyatt Regency; Fairmont; Nob Hill Lambourne; Harbour Court; Diva; Orchard.

CONTRIBUTORS
Series adviser: Melissa Shales   **Designer:** Design 23   **Copy editor:** Lynn Bresler
Verifier: Joanna Whitaker   **Researcher:** Caroline Alder   **Indexer:** Marie Lorimer